ROOTS and WINGS

A parents' guide to learning and
communicating with children
to forge a family
with mettle

Lili-Ann Kriegler

First published by Ultimate World Publishing 2022
Copyright © 2022 Lili-Ann Kriegler

ISBN

Paperback: 978-1-922714-85-5
Ebook: 978-1-922714-86-2

Lili-Ann Kriegler has asserted her rights under the Copyright, Designs and Patents Act 1988 to be identified as the author of this work. The information in this book is based on the author's experiences and opinions. The publisher specifically disclaims responsibility for any adverse consequences which may result from use of the information contained herein. Permission to use information has been sought by the author. Any breaches will be rectified in further editions of the book.

All rights reserved. No part of this publication may be reproduced, stored in or introduced into a retrieval system, or transmitted in any form, or by any means (electronic, mechanical, photocopying, recording or otherwise) without the prior written permission of the author. Any person who does any unauthorised act in relation to this publication may be liable to criminal prosecution and civil claims for damages. Enquiries should be made through the publisher.

Cover design: Ultimate World Publishing
Layout and typesetting: Ultimate World Publishing
Editor: Marinda Wilkinson

Ultimate World Publishing
Diamond Creek,
Victoria Australia 3089
www.writeabook.com.au

Testimonials

Our family first met Lili-Ann Kriegler 20 years ago when she taught our son at kindergarten and subsequently also taught our daughter. Lili-Ann was able to create strong working relationships with both children even though they had very different personalities and learning styles. She introduced them to age-appropriate critical thinking techniques and stretched them beyond what they believed were their capabilities. Lili-Ann also provided many tips for parents on raising children which were gratefully received. We have appreciated having her in our lives.

Jill Elias, Parent
Fintona Early Learning Centre

Under the guidance and with the enthusiasm and skill of Lili-Ann, my children were provided an ideal foundation for school readiness and beyond. Their early learning experience was a wonderful introduction to education, including creative and fun play in the areas of literacy, maths and science. On an emotional level, a healthy culture of respect and care for one another was embedded within a safe and calm environment with the encouragement of both group and individual interests.

Sharon A Kendall, Parent
Fintona Early Learning Centre

Lili-Ann is a wonderful inspiration and mentor who has helped shape our way of thinking in our workplace. Her commitment and vision for meaningful conversations in our work with young children has transformed our practice and supported us to stretch our minds, to look beyond the walls of our college and design programs that are authentic to the many different ways of thinking and knowing in our young learners and indeed in ourselves as educators. She is witty, knowledgeable and a pleasure to work with.

We look forward to extending our thinking and learning through this new publication.

Debbie Hendren, ELC Director &
Katina Grammatoglou, ELC Educational Leader
Presbyterian Ladies' College

Lili-Ann and I have worked and travelled together for Independent Schools Victoria for the past nine years. It has been a privilege to do so, and it is rare to meet someone as thoughtful and eloquent as Lili-Ann. She listens, thinks, then expresses ideas fluently, enabling those around her to learn, understand and grow as educators, therapists and parents. Due to her rich experience with children in the early years, the Feuerstein programs, the Reggio Emilia Approach, Bright Start and Systematic Concept Teaching, she possesses a wide base to draw upon. Nothing seems to faze her – she is always a sea of calm and a great team player.

Diane Bourke, Project Manager, Independent Schools Victoria &
Past Junior School Principal Melbourne Girls' Grammar School

Lili-Ann's knowledge and understanding of education, particularly early years, is vast. She has a rich and deep knowledge of the Reggio Emilia principles and practices and has been very closely involved with the dissemination of this approach in Australia, including having successfully headed an early learning centre where she implemented this philosophy. Lili-Ann continues to stretch boundaries and make the connections between theory and practice. She explores the links between emotion and cognition and how this plays out in the classroom. She seeks every opportunity to contribute to current research and further best practice. This, combined with her deep understanding and expertise in teaching, makes her an outstanding educator.

Genia Janover, Past Principal of Bialik College
Ambassador and Principal Advisor at Independent Schools Victoria

Lili-Ann Kriegler, in her career as an educator of both children and adults, has made an original and wide-reaching contribution to education in this country. Lili-Ann's personal gifts include a wonderful imagination and extraordinary creativity, combined with a strong curiosity and I have been privileged over many years to witness her work in primary school classrooms, as well as early childhood settings, including the design of a wonderful early childhood centre.

Recently in her role at Independent Schools Victoria, Lili-Ann instigated and maintained the stewardship of an innovative Thinker in Residence project, which culminated in an exhibition displayed in the Atrium at Federation Square, Melbourne. This event illustrates so well the special gifts of Lili-Ann and her ongoing innovative contribution to education in the early years across Australia.

Jan Millikan OAM, Educator, Author and Past President of the
Reggio Emilia Australian Information Exchange

We have been privileged to work and train with Lili-Ann for several years now. She has a warm and interactive presentation style, taking theoretical concepts and eloquently presenting them in a highly practical and structured way. Lili-Ann has wonderful communication skills: she listens, reflects, ponders and questions in a respectful and thoughtful way. She has extensive experience and expert knowledge about child development, especially during the early years and blends this knowledge, theory and practical experience in a very user-friendly way. This book will be an important and practical contribution to the literature for educators who seek to provide evidence-based, creative opportunities for their students.

Mary Williams, Guidance Officer, Prep Teacher and Feuerstein Trainer &
Jenny Cummings, Prep Co-ordinator and Feuerstein Trainer
Tamborine Mountain State School

I have had the pleasure of knowing Lili-Ann for several years. Upon meeting Lili-Ann I immediately saw that her understanding of education and children was vast and accomplished. She is perceptive, an observer, an active listener and a valued contributor.

We worked together on the Independent Schools Victoria (ISV) Arts Learning Festival in 2019. I appreciated Lili-Ann's support, enthusiasm and knowledge throughout this collaborative process. The Arts Learning Festival was a wonderful success which showcased and connected many of ISV's schools. I am grateful that we have maintained our connection.

I thoroughly enjoyed reading her first book, *Edu-Chameleon: Leverage 7 Dynamic Learning Zones to Enhance Young Children's Concept-Based Understanding*. The content resonated strongly with me and I discovered many provocations to implement in my work. I have recommended the book to many colleagues. I am looking forward to reading *Roots and Wings*. It is sure to offer incredible insights and information.

Claire Bartlett
Principal, Woodline Primary School, Geelong

Reviews

Lili-Ann Kriegler forges her place in the literary and arts world, through creating a performative foundry of metaphoric, poetic and pedagogical tools in her latest book, *Roots and Wings*.

Novelist, Booker Prize winner, and Sydney Peace Prize awardee, Arundhati Roy, suggests we take our place in the world and are not given it.

Through the pages of this compelling book, Lili-Ann draws on her experiences in the broad education field, to firmly take her own place and inspire others to do so.

Dr Avis Ridgway
Adjunct Research Associate, Faculty of Education, Monash University.

Lili-Ann Kriegler's book *Roots and Wings* contains powerful messages and practical advice on how to rear a family with mettle. Lili-Ann uses common sense, humour, anecdotes, quotes, learned educators' studies, psychology and philosophy to illustrate the themes that the family is the foundry which supports the child from birth to adulthood and that education and communication are the anvils upon which successful lives can be shaped. The family with mettle is closely bonded, high-functioning, strong and resilient and each child within the family is likely to be able to achieve their fullest potential of his or her talents and interests. Lili-Ann writes eloquently and builds her arguments in a readable, easy to follow manner. Many of her messages can be applied not just in raising children but in all aspects of life. Do not delay your gratification! This is a book to read now.

Jill Elias, Parent

Dedication

This book is dedicated to my parents, Bob and Bee Erasmus; siblings, Helene and Martin; husband, Pierre; and children, Sean and Candice.

You are the ones who make me whole – past, present and future.

Contents

Preface: Mettle Foundry ... 15
Introduction: Laying Down Strong Roots ... 21

Part A: Roots ... 33

Chapter One: Sense and Sensitivity. Infancy (birth to 18 months) ... 35

Chapter Two: The Unselfish Selfish Child. Toddlerhood (18 months to 3 years) ... 51

Chapter Three: Emerging from the Chrysalis. Preschool (3 to 5 years) ... 69

Chapter Four: A Shining Morning Face. Junior Primary (5 to 9 years) ... 97

Chapter Five: Beyond the Family: Stepping into the Neighbourhood. Senior Primary and Secondary (9 to 17 years) ... 147

Part B: Wings ... 165

Chapter Six: Taking Flight ... 167
Chapter Seven: The Hard Conversations ... 185
Chapter Eight: Forging a Family Culture ... 209
Afterword: Life as an Act of Creation ... 217
About the Author ... 221
Acknowledgements ... 225
References ... 229

Tiger

The Tyger

Tyger Tyger, burning bright,
In the forests of the night;
What immortal hand or eye,
Could frame thy fearful symmetry?

In what distant deeps or skies.
Burnt the fire of thine eyes?
On what wings dare he aspire?
What the hand, dare seize the fire?

And what shoulder, & what art,
Could twist the sinews of thy heart?
And when thy heart began to beat,
What dread hand? & what dread feet?

What the hammer? what the chain,
In what furnace was thy brain?
What the anvil? what dread grasp,
Dare its deadly terrors clasp!

When the stars threw down their spears
And water'd heaven with their tears:
Did he smile his work to see?
Did he who made the Lamb make thee?

Tyger Tyger burning bright,
In the forests of the night:
What immortal hand or eye,
Dare frame thy fearful symmetry?

WILLIAM BLAKE

Blacksmith foundry

PREFACE

Mettle Foundry

'Mettle: a person's ability to cope well with difficulties; spirit and resilience.'
Lexico online dictionary

This book is inspired by William Blake's poem, *The Tyger*.

Blake's words evoke an immense foundry, sparking with creative energy. A place where ideas are forged into substance. I visualise finely crafted, well-worn tools, feel the heat of the furnace and hear the clamour and hiss as metal is wrought into shape.

The metaphor of the blacksmith's workshop is central to this book about forging a family with mettle. Mettle is a proactive point of view and spirit of resilience you can adopt to give you and your family the best chance of life success. Blakes' poem is about a tiger, but I think he was talking about the wonder of all our creation.

I'm a trained educator and education consultant with a wide interest in all areas of learning. In the late 1990s I was on a course with a physiotherapist. We were studying anatomy. She held up her long, tapered fingers. Opening and closing her fist she said, 'There are 27 bones in this hand. It's a miracle of nature. I can't imagine how anyone thinks they've the right to harm someone or take a life. It's incomprehensible. People just don't understand how unique we all are in this universe.' This insight echoes in my consciousness all the time.

The human hand is made up of the wrist, palm and fingers, and does indeed have 27 bones. It also has 27 joints, 34 muscles, over 100 ligaments and tendons and a multitude of blood vessels and nerves (Orthopedics North West, 2021). And hands are only a small part of the human body.

What about the mind! If the hand is miraculous, there are really no words for the absolute astonishment of the human brain and mind. I don't equate the brain with the mind, but I do think that crafting the brain leads to the crafting of the mind. Mind and matter together are welded to form each person's unique identity and pathway in this life.

We who raise children can support the formation of their identity. However, it is not my contention that, as the Jesuits say, 'Give me a child until the age of seven and they will be mine for life.' I don't believe in creating a mini me. But I do believe that we have a role in who our children become.

If you've been involved in any artistic or crafting endeavour, you'll recognise the sense that the process and product push back. The task teaches itself to you and the outcome is more than the sum of the goal, task and process.

In my thirties I was obsessed with puppetry. I loved the art of it and the performance. I decided to create a dancing fairy one day who obstinately insisted on becoming a clown. I thought, 'Fine then, be a clown.' But when I tried to make it dance to the 'Nutcracker' music, it only wanted to dance to 'Scatman'! The puppet virtually wrote its own script. In the end, the show I created was exactly that: a dialogue between the puppeteer and the puppet.

If anyone has told this story exceptionally, it was the journalist, author and humourist Carlo Lorenzini, best known as Carlo Collodi, creator of *Pinocchio*. Geppetto, the craftsman makes a wooden puppet and his dream is for it to be a 'real boy'. In the story Pinocchio is sent to school but is lured off his path into many misadventures. There is a difference between school and the school of life.

To pick up on the central metaphor of this book, in the blacksmith's forge, a workpiece is used to craft artefacts. The workpiece is a block of amalgamated metal in a state between molten liquid and solidified metal. It is malleable. It may be used to create an ingot, which is the first step in the creation of the finished product.

I see our work with our children as similar to the process of creating ingots. The 'mettle' in our foundry workpiece is an amalgam of our aspirations, values, resources and contributions to their future. But the final shape, the artefact of their life, is entirely up to them. We do not have the power, and most likely don't have the will, to make our children in our image. Their world is, and continues to be, different from ours. But we can give them the best start we are able and support them on their journey when they leave ... and fly.

You are the bows from which your children
As living arrows are sent forth
The archer sees the mark upon the path of the infinite
And he bends you with his might
That his arrows may go swift and far
Let your bending in the archer's hand be for gladness
For even as he loves the arrow that flies
So he loves also the bow that is stable
Kahlil Gibran, The Prophet (1923)

Imagine in our foundry we have 'mettle' bow and arrows. The bow and arrow work together as a system. The family is a system. But it's not a closed system. As you grow with your family, your perceptions, values and beliefs will shift in response to everything you encounter together. Peter Senge first spoke about a system as a learning organisation in his book *The Fifth Discipline* (Senge, 2006) and the idea of lifelong shared learning resonates with me. Systems thinking sounds technical, but it has the power to change the culture of your family. Its future focus changes the questions you ask yourself. It changes the way you think and the way you speak. It directs your approach to parenting and to life. If we see our family as a system, however it is constituted in the modern world, we see beyond any given moment. We anticipate the consequences of our actions. We have the choice to proactively shape what is to come.

A nostalgia for the future

I travelled to northern Italy three times between 2000 and 2016 to attend education study tours at the internationally famous Reggio Emilia Infant-Toddler Centres and Preschools. During my sojourns, I encountered the term 'a nostalgia for the future'. The educators described it as a motivational force when planning their work with young children. It puzzled me for years. But over time, it has become one of the most meaningful ideas acquired through my teacher studies.

Nostalgia was first coined as a term during the late 1600s when Swiss mercenaries abroad displayed extreme homesickness. The malady was named by Johannes Hofer, a medical student, as nostalgia after the Greek 'nostos' for homecoming and 'algos' for pain or longing. That sounds quite depressing! But over time, the meaning of nostalgia has changed. In recent decades it has come to be appreciated as an emotion which allows individuals to remember personally meaningful and rewarding experiences from the past. Nostalgia triggers a sense of belonging, personal meaning and self-esteem (Routledge, 2016).

Who hasn't sat around the dinner table listening to a family member recounting some story probably shared a million times over? But we still love it. We roar with laughter at familiar antics and anecdotes. And if we're good, we won't butt in and deliver the punchline! As we listen, we line up one of our favourite stories to recount. Or we might remind everyone about a great family recipe, a favourite childhood destination, a moment when one of the tribe achieved something noteworthy. What I call podium moments. When someone has worked hard for something and it has paid off.

These stories, memories and the emotions embedded in them, are family glue – the ties that bind.

If we unpicked the stories, we would also find they resonate with the personal, familial and cultural values that are closely held and lived out by each of us.

So how does all this relate to a nostalgia for the future? I think the Reggio Emilia educators are conscious of creating a kind of learning that will be looked back on as having been formative, foundational, connective, imaginative, intriguing, influential, value-laden and diverse.

So, a nostalgia for the future of a family is when in decades' time we might look back with the knowledge that conscious care was taken to forge its success. That the right elements were in place to bring cohesion, collaboration, care and competence.

I'm not crazy enough to think that we can plot out our future meticulously and that we can be assured it will come out exactly as planned. Life is just too unpredictable, varied, complicated and hard for that. But just because it is all those things, it doesn't mean we can't have a red-hot go at creating the kind of family we want and influencing how we'd like to live our lives and how we'd like to see our children succeed.

No matter how far along you are on your tumultuous parental journey, I am sure your primary goal is to forge a family with mettle. One that is closely bonded, high-functioning, strong and resilient.

That will never happen by accident!

This book outlines how you might craft positive interactions moment to moment – because in each moment, the golden thread of the future is being forged.

INTRODUCTION

Laying Down Strong Roots

'To invent your own life's meaning is not easy, but it's still allowed and I think you'll be happier for the trouble.'
Bill Watterson
American cartoonist (Calvin and Hobbes)

This book is for parents and all other primary caregivers. It explores how education and communication are the vehicles for developing family cohesion. The substance of your communication becomes the substance of your family. Good communication is based on good thinking. Good thinking is based on good education.

My parents, Bob and Bee Erasmus, never stopped emphasising the value of education. They said that it was something my siblings and I could never be robbed of and which would form the basis of who we might become. My father always said that education gave us *roots and wings* and this idea has been so formative in my life.

I researched this phrase and it appears to have come into use in 1953 from a prominent New York newspaper editor, Hodding Carter who credited it to 'an anonymous wise woman' in his book, *Where the Main Street Meets the River*. The timing is about right for my father to have come across it. He was an avid reader and Readers' Digest subscriber.

The image on the cover of this book is a deliberate synthesis of a forged metallic root and tree structure with natural leaves sprouting from it. The metallic part is your parental lived experience and family culture, the sprouting represents the unconstrained uniqueness of each child.

The metallic roots reach into your own experience and value system as a parent. Your roots soaked up ideas and knowledge that supported your growth. This is the perspective you pass on to your children, but they are free to do with it what they will. Hopefully, they feel so well nourished and nurtured that your tree creates seeds with wings. I like to imagine those wonderful seeds that look like helicopter rotors, lifting off in the summer breeze and landing in new soil of their own, to start their own independent lives. And hopefully forge a new family with its own unique culture.

Helicopter seed

The early education and communication you provide and share with your children is their soil bed. If it is rich in support, love, stimulation, resources and language, the child will flourish. If the child is deprived of all these elements, they will languish.

Maslow's hierarchy of needs

The renowned American psychologist, Abraham Maslow (1908–1970) succinctly captured the essence of human needs, from the most basic to the most sophisticated and aspirational.

He proposed five layers. From the bottom to the top, they are:

- Physiological needs – what we need to survive: air, water, food, shelter, clothing, reproduction
- Safety needs – personal security, employment, resources, health, property
- Love and belonging – family, closeness, connection, friendship
- Esteem – respect, self-esteem, status, recognition, strength, freedom
- Self-actualisation – becoming the most that one can be.

Maslow defined self-actualisation as achieving the fullest use of one's talents and interests – the need 'to become everything that one is capable of becoming' (Maslow, 2017).

When you are looking down into the face of a newborn infant, you will hardly be thinking about Abraham Maslow or self-actualisation. (Well, you might … but no you won't.) You will most likely be awe-struck and speechless because of the miracle you hold in your arms.

However, even though you may not be conscious of it, everything you believe about what is important in life is already part of that moment. The circumstances of the child's arrival, your past experiences, your relationships, your belief systems and your expectations will influence his or her path towards self-actualisation.

(Just to be clear, I am highly aware of gender equity, and respect parents' rights around how they regard and address their children. But for ease of expression, I will use 'his' and 'her' throughout this book.)

There is a wealth of research indicating that children's early experiences impact on and predict later academic, social and professional success. It starts with children having nurturing, caring parental relationships, and extends to the range and quality of experiences young children are exposed to as they grow up. The child's brain is 90% developed by the time they are five years old and these early years are a critical time for learning. The studies on early brain development show how positive interactions bolster positive self-esteem, and conversely negative circumstances can play out negatively in a child's life.

This book is not about standing on a soapbox telling everyone what will happen if they don't do what I present for consideration – but I am in the business of focusing on the positives.

There will be parents who are in a comfortable situation and others who may not be in a great place. Everyone has different resources, conditions, environments, financial constraints, family realities. What I ask everyone to do, is focus on what can be done for children to create positive experiences in whatever way it can be done.

Experience creates neural networks

Not everyone loves biology, so if you don't want to read the about brain cells, skip to the next section ...

The brain cells, or networks of neurons, are the roots of learning. They even look like roots!

The brain is the only organ that is created from both inside and outside us. And this is for our own survival. Life is a human lottery and none of us knows what we'll have to deal with once we find ourselves on the planet. We need to learn as we go. But we don't come unprepared – we have billions of brain cells and they are ready to create trillions of connections. As we experience the world, we make meaning from what we are sensing. We don't only record experience; we internalise and order that experience in a unique way. The way we construct our own perceptions and meaning is what makes us all unique individuals (Shore, 1997).

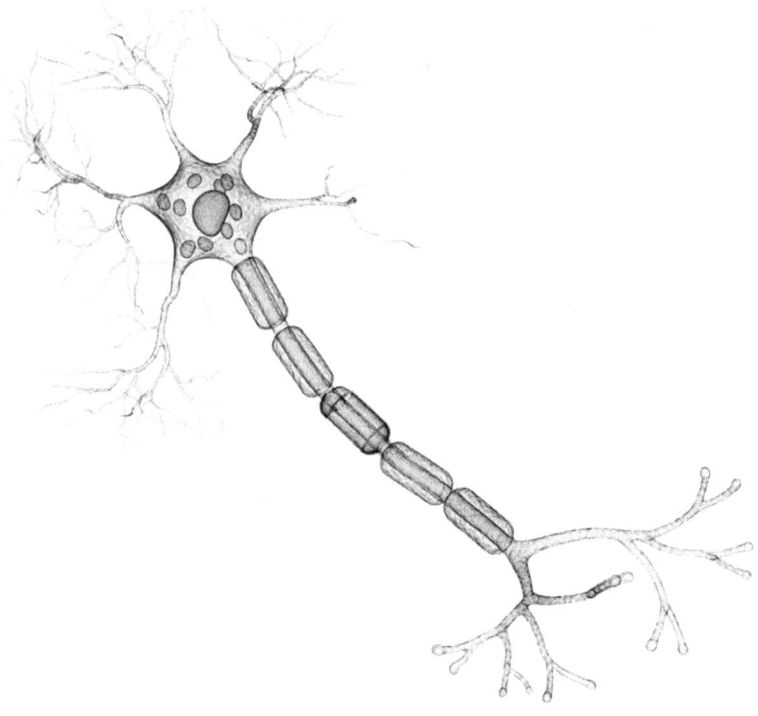

Neuron

Neurons are composed of a cell body (soma), axon and dendrites. Each neuron communicates with another at a point of contact called the synapse. The more regularly and strongly a signal fires between neurons, the more the axons become myelinated. That is, they are covered by myelin, a white fatty substance, that speeds up the messages.

Brain plasticity and neuronal growth rely on rich stimulation. As Donald Hebb, Canadian psychologist wrote when he studied neural assemblages in the brain, 'what fires together, wires together' (Hebb, 1949). He discovered that repeated stimulation of connected neurons, made them stronger and capable of more efficient communication.

Understanding this and recognising the mechanism for maximising neuronal efficiency explains why varied experience and rich, intentional learning environments optimise young children's learning, both in the home and in early educational settings.

Experience is the way the child absorbs information from and communicates with the world beyond his or her own body. Who we are; and who we will become, is dependent on our interaction with the environment, our relationship with others in the world and the internal workings of our own brains. Each person develops a unique network.

And this is already being laid down in infancy!

So just as healthy roots are the basis of a healthy plant, a healthy neuronal network is the basis of a flourishing child.

The child is at the centre of nested social circles

Language is not learned by anyone in isolation, it is a social phenomenon. As children grow and develop, the range and variety of their interactions change. Their contacts and community expand and they are exposed to wider and wider influences. The late, renowned psychologist, Urie Bronfenbrenner, developed an ecological model which shows this social expansion in a series of concentric circles (Bronfenbrenner, 1979). Children are influenced by their encounters with actors in each of these circles as they grow out into to the world.

It is good to be aware of this right from the outset. You're not going to always be in control of what your child hears, sees, is exposed to or experiences. And with the explosion of digital communication, this is truer than ever. So, the more you can do to support your child into becoming a good thinker early on, the better.

Throughout the book I will refer to Maslow's idea of self-actualisation. He envisions it as a state of autonomy, the ability to take flight. It doesn't happen in one monumental leap when a person reaches adulthood, it is slowly constructed along the way. I think of it being made up of components which develop separately but coalesce into one. The components are self-regulation, self-esteem, self-purpose, self-mastery, creativity and contribution. You will come across these words throughout this book because they'll help to forge each participant in a family's ability to collaborate in a resilient, high-functioning way.

Despite most of these words starting with 'self', a person on the path to self-actualisation moves beyond a focus on self. Maslow indicates that they have rich personal relationships and a 'freshness of appreciation' for all life can offer. He talks about community feeling, a sense of oneness with humanity captured in the German word 'Gemeinschaftsgefühl' (Wikipedia, 2021). Beyond their own interests, it is most likely you wish your children to live a life of contribution to others as well as to themselves. To reach a state of self-transcendence.

Be an 'I have' person

Dr Judith Paphazy, a highly respected Melbourne psychologist, delivered a talk in 2000 when I was teaching at Bialik College, which has stayed with me for decades. She said that children only need one 'I have' person in their life to make a difference. And she told us that as teachers, or parents, we could be that 'I have' person. This is a person the child can trust without fear, knowing that they have their back. Someone they can trust and continue to trust to become resilient. Her talk was at once humbling and inspiring.

The biographical novel *Hillbilly Elegy* (Vance, 2016) is a testament to this idea in which J.D. Vance acknowledges the role of his grandmother, Mamaw, in having his back throughout his youth.

But let's cycle back to the newborn. Right from the beginning, when children are born they are being bombarded by sensations. In the words of Willam James, often called the father of psychology, babies are born in a 'blooming, buzzing confusion' (James, 2021). Perhaps even before they are born, they are responding to the stimuli around them. And yes, at first you are a stimulus, and hopefully a big, warm hugging stimulus that regularly supplies food, comfort, shelter, a cot and cute clothes. As the days and weeks pass, you will coalesce into a mum, dad or other recognisable primary caregiver!

Positive early interactions are like deposits in the baby's trust bank. Having needs met, having regular experiences that accumulate towards predictable routines are part of the attachment and sense of belonging a child needs to feel safe and secure.

If the needs on the lower levels of Maslow's hierarchy are not met, it is much harder to get to the place where as an older person, he or she will develop self-esteem or reach upwards towards a plane of self-actualisation.

Helping your children be their best

In essence, this book is about recognising the potential in every day for positive interactions with your kids that will help them be their best. In the first part we'll look at the different education stages and the modes of communication most important in each. This includes the development of language, conceptual understanding and cognition from birth to adolescence. It is a bottom up perspective, exploring what is needed to create a robust family by supporting education through continually emerging stages of development. During the discussion on education I will regularly refer to aspects of communication. In truth, education and communication go hand in hand.

Communication is complex and includes many forms and layers. It is broadly either non-verbal or verbal. In the non-verbal category, I'll refer to gesture and non-verbal expression through movement and the arts. In verbal communication, I'll talk about pitch and tone, vocalisation and spoken language. These non-verbal and verbal elements are present in childhood, stretch through adolescence, and continue on into adulthood. But they have different emphases and complexities at different ages. Communication is more than language; communication informs our lives.

In the five chapters of Part A, I focus on practical aspects of education, communication and the mechanics of learning language from babyhood to the neighbourhood. No child develops at the exact same pace, so the age ranges might vary in your family, but roughly children will go through each of these on their way to adolescence. You will be at different stages of parenting and your children will be at different ages, but it is worthwhile reading through all the stages, just to get the full picture. Clearly this book is also for grandparents who find themselves on this journey for a second time, with their grandchildren!

Through the five age ranges, your child will pass through several expanding communities as mentioned above and depicted in the graphic organiser that follows. You will have less and less immediate influence, but the soil bed you provide early on will resonate more strongly if you have prepared it with care.

Urie Bronfenbrenner: Ecological Model

The second part of the book presents a more philosophical and psychological perspective on family culture. I describe some of the issues facing young people today and share ideas about how to forge a positive culture to bolster resilience.

To help our children fly high and be what they are meant to be!

PART A

Roots

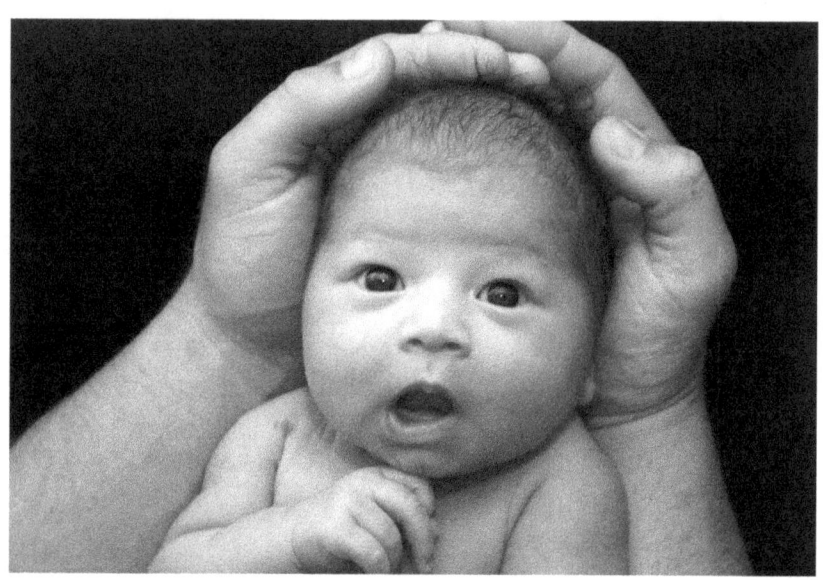

Infants

CHAPTER ONE

Sense and Sensitivity Infancy (birth to 18 months)

'The senses, being the explorers of the world, open the way to knowledge.'
Maria Montessori

At no time is sensory information more important than in infancy.

Early sensory experiences including holding, touching, nursing, feeding and caring are foundational forms of communication. The infant is prelingual and so relies on these sensory means of communication.

The pressure as you hold them, the sound of your voice as you coo and chat, the way you make eye contact, your smell (in a good way) and what they taste when you are near them all blend into a combinatory experience of the world.

Across the world, there are different ways of holding, rocking, swaddling, carrying and feeding babies, but this early experience is the basis of attachment.

'Sense' is a great word, because it is what you receive from the world via your senses, but it also encompasses meaning. When you combine sensation with meaning, you get perception. Perception is a higher level of sensing, because the infant is starting to interpret what they are experiencing. It is the beginning of cognition. They interpret patterns to make meaning. They might hear a door open, and expect a person to appear. They hear you shaking the milk bottle and anticipate being fed. They accidentally knock the mobile above their cot, hear a tinkle of bells, and in time they can do this on purpose. If the baby wasn't interpreting the patterns, and encoding these regular and accidental occurrences, they wouldn't be learning. But they are. Their brains are working faster than any computer and they're building the networks of sensory memories we mentioned earlier, which store massive amounts of cumulative information about the world.

The 'sensitivity' of the chapter title is *your awareness* that all this is going on. If you are sensitive to what is occurring in your baby's world, you can put things in place, and use your communication for the best outcomes right from the start. And doing that is important! When you respond to Maslow's base needs like satisfying hunger, warmth and security, you are giving the baby the message that they are significant. Their existence is recognised and nurtured.

Tragic studies of children in deprived conditions indicate if this recognition doesn't happen babies languish, stop communicating and even die. When the baby's needs are met and they feel a sense of approval, there is a release of growth hormone which is vital for the child to thrive (Johnson, et al., 2010) in (Greenfield, 2015).

Having a stimulating environment and rich interactive experiences can have positive effects into adulthood. A research study started in 1970, in which children from six weeks onwards received stimulating interactions and educational experiences for five years, shows brain enhancement in the frontal cortex of adults four decades later (Farah, 2021). Research shows other positive changes too. The cell body size increases as does brain weight. There is a proliferation of the dendrites which communicate with other cells and all this together means there is a greater surface area to the network (Greenfield, 2015).

What does this mean for parenting and communication at this early stage?

Focal area of development

As suggested, key information at this time is through the senses. So, touch, sound, sights, smells and taste are all important. Sight, motion and hearing are key contributors to language learning. None of these happen in isolation. They work together all the time. For simplicity I will discuss them separately below.

Seeing eye to eye
The most important act of communication from birth is having eye contact. It is the earliest 'conversation' you have with your newborn. Babies learn from you. If you search for and value eye contact, they will too. Eye contact is a vital part of creating attachment. The late renowned psychologist, Jerome Bruner, saw these very early interactions as 'a predictable format of interaction that can serve as a microcosm for communicating and for constituting a shared reality' (Bruner, 1983). The give and take of early communication are predictors and precursors to

how all our communication is part of a mutuality in relationships. The pattern of communication, which is transactional, shared, interconnective, purposeful, mutually given and received is already intrinsic to seeing eye to eye with an infant.

Jack Schonkoff, neuroscientist, calls it 'serve and return' (Schonkoff, 2021); and Roberta Golinkoff and Kathy Hirsh-Pasek, language researchers, call it a 'conversational duet' (Golinkoff, 2015). This is especially so when it is combined with the sing-song style of communication so characteristic when we 'talk' to babies.

Disturbingly, there is evidence now that mobile phones and devices are interfering with this essential early eye contact. Even when a child is nursing, being bottle fed, pushed in a pram or being minded and cared for in other ways, devices are coming between the parent and the child (Christakis, 2021). You will read in a moment or two about the importance of facial expression. The interruption of early eye contact with devices not only leaves the child in a non-communicative space, but it also short-circuits his or her ability to mirror and internalise eye contact and facial expression with all its crucial emotional messaging. I say this knowing that my adult children regularly express relief that the mobile phone was not around when they were growing up, because mine appears physically attached to my person! I know how compelling these devices can be.

Facial expression
As we have eye contact with babies, combined with vocalisation and facial expression, they start attuning to the emotional qualities of the relationship you are forging with them. They will later use what they have 'recorded' from watching your face, to modulate their own emotions and relationships. If you are predictable in your interactions, they learn to feel trusting and secure.

In a 'still face' experiment, Dr Edward Tronick, Director of the Child Development Centre at Harvard University researched how important expression is in natural interaction with babies. In a YouTube video (Tronick, 2009), you can see how a baby reacts when her mum stops her normal responsiveness and replaces it with a kind of blank face. The baby becomes visibly distressed. When an adult is responsive to an infant, they learn about emotions, social engagement, and other elements of communication. When the mum's responsiveness is interrupted, the infant becomes overwrought and tries in several of the usual, already learned ways to regain the attention and connection of the relationship. Secure and successful interactions with positive facial expressions is key to a child's development of trust through a healthy sense of attachment. Attachment theory, researched by John Bowlby, of the Royal College of Psychiatrists, suggests that children who do not experience strong attachment at an early age, can display many problems of disconnection, negative self-image and behavioural difficulties later in life (Bowlby, 1977).

Hand-eye coordination
Any baby book (I was addicted to Penelope Leach's book, *Baby and Child* when I had my two children), will tell you that routine is important. But routine is not about strictly following the advice you read in the books! It's about finding out who your baby is, what he or she likes or thrives on, and how you harmonise together. Once you establish early interaction, some predictability and regularity will help your child to feel settled and secure. The sights, sounds, experiences and sensations start to make sense because they occur in a regular pattern. Now, having had two babies with colic myself and living through the early settling experiences, I know this predictability sounds too good to be true. There is a time in the afternoon when you might fantasise about a potent purple cocktail to weather the pressure. Sleepless nights lead to exhausted parents and bubs. And exhaustion makes feeding, bathing, colic, niggles and demands even more difficult. But after a time, things do seem to settle down.

At the very beginning, babies literally don't know what *they* are, or what *you* are. Until eight weeks they are short-sighted and don't use their hands unless you place something in them.

Besides chatting to your baby and cooing conversationally (yes, you do it!), you can encourage him or her to look at something within the range of focus, which is about the length of a ruler. Don't move it around too quickly because it'll be too difficult to follow.

As the babies get older, they start to grasp things like rattles. There is period of months during which the baby learns the eye-hand coordination to reach for, touch and grasp objects. You can help this eye-hand coordination and depth perception by offering mobiles early on which hang above the child, then offer stable objects to reach for. When your baby is reaching for an object, don't short-circuit this motion by placing it in the hand before he or she has touched it. This range finding is part of the development of hand-eye coordination.

By about six months, babies are good at reaching for, grasping and holding anything they find. And without fail, they will put them in their mouths!

Babbling conversations
Hearing combines with touch and vision to enable babies to make sense of the world.

Early on, your baby will start to babble, vocalise and become very 'talkative'. If you have the opportunity to watch the conversation of toddlers on phones on YouTube (funnyplox, 2021) you will notice across the board, that despite the fact infant children don't have a real vocabulary yet, they display a sophisticated idea of how conversations are held in day-to-day life. They pause between vocalisations, waiting for a 'response'. There is a tonal quality and a rhythm in what and how they speak to a real or imaginary person. Besides all this they display facial expressions, movement and mannerisms they have observed. Some hold the phone to their ears, but others talk into the phone as though it's in speaker mode. Some of those who are up and walking even pace the floor the way we adults do.

The sophistication they display is because they are mirroring your voice patterns and the social aspects of what you're saying to them. You're not only imprinting language, but also cultural mores and practices related to communication. They pick up the phonetics and the intentional, emotional qualities in the tone when you speak. Tonality and rhythm are like music and words are like lyrics. The meaning is conveyed by both. And babies get the music first.

Talking with your hands
We all talk with our hands every day – in some cultures people do double the amount than in others! When your infant is under 18 months (and later) your words and your gestures combine to assist with meaning making. Pointing, presenting objects, motion, touch, modelling and demonstration all assist the child to interpret meaning. Along with facial expression, all your other gestures are key communications for you baby.

Between a year and 18 months some children say their first words. These might be 'mama', 'dada', or other simple words. Initially the words refer to something – like to you. But as the child engages socially more and more, these words might even be framed as questions. The child might refer to a dog as 'da'. Or they might see the dog running and say 'da' meaning 'what is the dog doing?', or 'where is the dog going?'

Supporting communication

Talk, read and sing
There are many ways to support this early language development. In her book *Thirty Million Words*, Dana Suskind, a paediatric surgeon and researcher, lists three ways to do this: tune in, talk more and take turns (Suskind, 2015) . Suskind's interest in early language development grew out of her work doing cochlear implants. After the operations she visited homes and found that in some of the families her patients and their hearing siblings were being exposed to a lot more language than

others. The children who were exposed to more words and a more sophisticated quality of language were discovered to be more successful in many situations including school, social settings and in later life. On the basis of her observations, she connected with the research of Betty Hart and Todd Risley (Hart & Risley, 1995) who had determined that in some cases by the age of four, some children had heard 30 million more words that other children in families where parents did not speak to the children as regularly. Suskind wrote the book to encourage parents and teachers everywhere to use rich language around young children.

If you watched the television program *Orange is the New Black* you'll have heard how Maria Ruiz reveals to her boyfriend, Yadriel, that she is being sent to another prison much further away. She begs Yadriel that he 'must speak to Pepa so that the baby doesn't have language difficulties in the future'. The very next time Yadriel comes to visit, he is shown speaking much more to the baby, showing he has listened to Maria's request (Fandom, 2021) .This interlude is not accidental and the TV corporation Univision has teamed up with the Clinton Foundation's initiative, 'Too Small to Fail', whose mission is to lead public awareness and an action campaign to promote the importance of early brain and language development and to empower parents with tools to talk, read, and sing with their young children from birth. Univision has been sowing seeds like this in other programs too. They even offer online resources for families (Clinton Foundation, 2021).

Tune in
Tuning in means taking note of what your child is focusing on and starting your 'conversation' from there. Craft the comments to the context. It is a kind of shared gaze – focusing on what has caught your child's attention. Because the child's experience is mostly focused on the outside world, it's hardly worth talking about what is in the other room if your child is focused on a fuzzy bee soft toy hanging about her head. When you say, 'buzzy bee', the infant starts to connect the sound to the object. Soon, if you say, 'buzzy bee', the baby will turn their gaze to it. But they've got

to 'know' about it because you followed their gaze first. Of course, you can also tell them that you are warming up their mush in the kitchen, but they won't be able to visualise it. They will, however, still be picking up on the music of your language.

Talk more
Talk more is adding gestures, facial expressions and rich vocabulary around the subject at hand. Embroidering what you say by adding the names of things, explaining things and extending conversations gives fuel to developing language. Back to buzzy bee. 'Buzzy bee is coming to say hello' as you move the toy towards the baby. 'Feel how soft buzzy bee is.' 'Do you want to hold buzzy bee?' 'Buzzy bee is flying up, up, up.' (I know, tell me to stop! But you have to expand the language in context.)

Taking turns
Taking turns is exactly what it means – share the conversation. Create pauses as though your child could respond in fully formed language, even if it is only a coo, babble, or even a burp.

Your child might start with 10 words at 18 months and have a vocabulary of 200 words a year later.

Talk to your baby all the time. Tell them what you're doing as you go through the normal routines. When you dress him, tell him what garments you're putting on. When you're washing her, let her know which parts of her body are getting soaped or dried.

You don't have to dumb down your language, just use your normal sentence structures. We saw earlier that infants who aren't even walking can mimic the conversational patterns we use.

Early words, word frames and set variations
Word frames and set variations sound technical, but they are familiar and you do them all the time. The description below is just to make

you more aware of them. Word frames provide a context or cue, that is familiar to introduce new words. So, a word frame might be 'look at the ... '. You can look at the dog, the light, the car, the moon and a thousand other things. The word frame tunes the child in that you are introducing something to attend to. Others might be: 'we are going to ... ', or '(child's name) likes ... ', or 'this is a ... '.

Set variations do the same cuing and tuning in, but they go on for a little longer and they repeat the same idea in a variety of ways. For example, you might say, 'Noah, bring the teddy to Mummy. Bring me the teddy. Give it to Mummy. Thank you, Noah, you gave Mummy the teddy.'

In this repetition the child is alerted to the grammar of pronouns like 'it' and 'me', as well as using the past tense. The teddy is either the subject or the object of the sentence (Bronson & Merryman, 2009). Even if you don't know the grammatical terminology, and I find it confusing at the best of times, we all follow the rules. In set variations you are passing on vocabulary and grammar at the same time.

Games and fun routines
We all know the game of peek-a-boo. There are several reasons why this game is important. The first is that it develops predictability, because the infant learns that whatever is hidden away will appear again and it paves the way for the child to understand object permanence. This is when a child might ask 'where da?' meaning, 'where is the dog' even when the pet is out of sight.

For reasons I don't understand and regret, nursery rhymes seem to be out of fashion. My babies loved 'Ride a cock-horse to Banbury Cross' while rocking on my knee, rowing the boat, or marching up and down the hill with the Duke of York. The predictable motion and sing-song sound of the words all add to the give and take of language experience.

Reading to your baby

In her book, *Reading Magic*, Mem Fox explains why reading to babies is important and on her website she has 10 commandments about doing it (Fox, 2008). I loved reading to my babies and two of my favourite early reading authors were Richard Scarry who created intricate picture books and Dick Bruna. Reading to children early starts to develop their awareness of books and written language. It is such a huge part of our culture and watching us turn pages, pointing and saying words out loud imprints the way books work.

Arranging the environment

Spending time in varied safe environments is important. Sleeping, playing, feeding, bathing, being outdoors and going beyond the house are all great for babies.

In each location, focus on security first. A calm baby is a receptive baby. If an infant is stressed, it's near impossible to get them to focus on anything other than how they are feeling. Their emotions aren't under their control and they come upon them in a giant wave.

When in the bath, for instance, babies might be traumatised by the water. The attempt to make them feel better by dangling a rattle of lively coloured plastic keys above their heads won't be effective. The toy won't distract them while they feel insecure. Maybe your infant needs to be cleaned with a warm facecloth rather than being immersed in the water or wrapped snugly in a towel and then dipped into the bath.

When indoors make sure there are toys within reach to amuse them as they learn to grasp and hold things. When my kids were sitting and crawling, their favourite place to play was the Tupperware cupboard. It was down low and the whole collection was regularly sprawled all over the kitchen floor. I'm surprised they aren't world champion frisbee players the way they threw the lids around! Bowls were converted into drums when they had a wooden spoon added to the ensemble, and they spent ages fitting one container into another.

You know this already: don't underestimate the joy of a carboard box! Yes, you bought a huge truck, you presented it with great expectations – and the first thing your kid does was crawl or toddle around it into the box. They love nothing more than climbing into it and playing 'hide and seek'. This action is extremely valuable because it teaches them about themselves, their size, shape and substance. In fact, this is a known schema of activity called *enclosure and enveloping* (Atherton & Nutbrown, 2013).

Mirrors are marvellous additions to their play space. Ensuring that they are safe or unbreakable, put mirrors on the floor where children can examine themselves as they sit or crawl, or place standing mirrors where they can see themselves waving stuff around or joyfully verbalising. Seeing their own images helps to develop their sense of identity.

Activities, outings and practical ideas

When my husband Pierre and I went out to dinners, we took our children, born five years apart, along with us. I made sleeping bags that had insulated bases so they could be placed in a pram or on the ground. They had two layers of covering, a thin inner zip-up layer for warm days or evenings and a second snugger outer-zip layer for warmth. The kids were perfectly happy to go into their sleeping bags under our chairs, a table or in a quiet corner where they could still see and hear us. I won't divulge how old they were the last time they still did this ... um, 14!

I was at a café the other day. Parents had brought their infant of about 18 months who was just on the verge of walking. The child sat on the dad's knee as he sipped his latte (I am in Melbourne after all). The mum had deftly and inconspicuously cut the dad's smashed avocado on toast into neat bite-size pieces, so he only needed one hand to eat. After the little boy had his own toast and drink (yes it may have been a Baba chino) he turned to a small suitcase which, when opened, revealed an obviously well-loved collection of café toys. Small cars, a bigger plastic cement truck, a six-piece puzzle and a small hard cover book of animals. It was peaceful, convivial and there was such an evident sense of routine and bonding.

You're roaring with laughter, aren't you? I know not all kids are as suggestible as this. If your little one is more active, you might have to implement what I call *mini journeys of discovery*. Even if you are on your own (but it's easier with extra hands), get up every 15 minutes and move around with the bub. Say hello to a waiter or other person. Everyone loves a baby. Show them a few things. Collect something, maybe a paper straw, serviette, spoon or anything handy. Talk about it as you go back to your seat and continue your own enjoyment as the baby is briefly entertained with the new object. Adjusting our expectations to a baby's attention span, tolerance and needs with mini plans like this makes all outings much easier.

Going to cafés, friends' homes, out to Grandma and Grandpa's are all great outings, even if these things can only happen at the weekends due to work commitments.

If your child is in a care setting, the same principles of care, responsiveness and stimulation should apply. With the extensive regulations in Australia, most centres are well-run and well-prepared to care for your child. But be aware of how your baby is responding when being dropped off and collected and develop open communication with the educators.

If your child is in full-time care, then the time you do have with them becomes extremely precious. Small joyful routines at home, quality 'conversation' with the serve and return described earlier and reading may be hard to fit in, but the benefits are worthwhile. It's the quality of the time spent together, not the quantity that counts in the end.

IN SUMMARY:

- Infancy is a foundational time for attachment, security and communication
- Babies rely on their senses to experience and interpret what is happening around them
- Communication commences with eye contact and facial expression
- Listening to the human voice attunes the baby to the fluency, pitch and tone of language
- Routine care and conversation encourage the child to use their own bodies and voices to explore the world
- Human brains are developed from stimulation both within and beyond the body
- Constellations and patterns of infant experiences allow the baby to predict events and recognise entities and objects in the world around them
- Beyond simple sensing, babies develop perception, the early cognition which is a combination of experience and meaning
- Babies' worlds are given meaning with caring adults' own words, gestures, facial expressions, demonstrations and explanations which they learn to imitate over time
- Having a rich, stimulating environment has positive effects on later social, scholastic and professional success
- A combination of security and stimulation is helpful in all environments, from staying at home to moving out into the world.

Toddlers

CHAPTER TWO

The Unselfish Selfish Child Toddlerhood (18 months to 3 years)

'It's no use going back to yesterday, because I was a different person then.'
Alice in Wonderland
Lewis Carroll

I can't believe I've got to Chapter Two without mentioning the internationally famous Swiss psychologist Jean Piaget. Piaget's groundbreaking research saw children's thought processes as being qualitatively different from adults' thinking and he categorised the development into four stages:

sensorimotor (birth–2 years), preoperational (2–7 years), concrete operational (7–11 years) and formal operational (12 and up). The word 'operation' refers to a mental task the developing child can do in his or her mind, and they go up in complexity and abstraction as the child matures.

The age group 18 months to three years is crossing over from sensorimotor to preoperational. After reading Chapter One on infants, you will know that *sensory* relates to incoming signals through the senses and *motor* refers to movement and locomotion. Preoperational means that despite the child's growing recognition of things around them and even being able to name multiple objects, he or she doesn't have the capacity yet to do complex thinking or use a high level of logic. And we have to be aware of this when we interact with toddlers and small children. It can be hard work, because they are becoming more and more knowledgeable and adventurous, but their understanding of how things relate to one another isn't well-established. In a phrase, they can't see the consequences. It's our role to help them connect the dots. And we need to do this while we keep them safe from their own curiosity as intrepid adventurers.

Focal area of development

Naming and recognising objects in the here and now

In the preoperational stage, the most significant thing that occurs, as mentioned, is that toddlers are more able to identify things. Language develops very quickly. They are constantly putting words, or labels to objects, events, persons and processes. They use single worlds and start to string two or more words together. By three, some children are using coherent sentences.

They identify things in pictures too. They can even learn to identify what they haven't encountered in real life yet, in pictures! I mentioned Richard Scarry earlier. My children learned to name hundreds of things from those picture books. This is remarkable because it's symbolic thinking. The word dog, or the picture of a dog *represents* a real dog. When the child knows about a dog, they start to be able to *think* about one, even when it's not visible. In effect, the child is starting to generalise a schema for dog. That is, it's a mental category that they can add other dogs to and know that they share similar features. Initially, they might think all dogs are small and fluffy, like the legendary book hero Tintin's Snowy. But they will expand this schema as they encounter more dogs, perhaps the *101 Dalmatians*?

As we grow up, this facililty of holding things as schemas in our minds, is what makes us unique on the planet and has resulted in the sophisticated, engineered, technological world we live in. Einstein developed his theory of relativity purely by manipulating ideas in his mind! (Do you understand it? I don't! You might be a scientist and able to explain why it's had a profound effect on our lives.) I'm not suggesting that your toddler, Gemma, is developing an historically influential theory in her mind ... yet. Toddlers' ability to understand symbols like words and pictures is the beginning of later complex abstract thinking. But their thinking is very situated in the here and now.

Todders are described as egocentric

Toddlers and small children are focused on themselves and their immediate sensations and experiences. In psychological terms they are described as being 'egocentric'. This is not the normal meaning of the word as self-obsessed or selfish. It makes sense that while children are still learning who they are, what they feel and what happens in their world, that they are less inclined to focus on and understand others. But that doesn't mean you can't lay down the foundations for understanding and feeling empathy for others.

I have stood in a three-year-old kinder room, where a child spilt his drink, and his friend said, 'never mind', took his hand and walked to where the water jug and cups were situated for children to help themselves.

That individual act counteracts the idea that children are entirely self-focused. The action indicates the child has absorbed a patient, supportive behaviour pattern from people around him. He might not be consciously deciding to do it, but he is mimicking what he's experienced from others.

The egocentrism in toddlers is not 'selfish' in the way we use it for adults or older children. When children are learning language, they cannot immediately understand it fully. They use words like *good, naughty, promise, love, share* and *doing favours* but don't yet have a genuine understanding of them. Your child might promise to be kind to the dog, but not understand that means not pulling its tail!

Even making a choice, which seems easy for us, can be very difficult for a toddler. They don't have the full reasoning power to deliberate and compare what the outcome of each choice will be and how it will affect them. When you offer them a choice, make it really simple like, 'Do you want to use the blue crayon, or the red crayon first?' Or if there are more crayons, 'Which colour would you like to use first?' 'Which will you eat first, the tomato of the cucumber?' (Or as my daughter, Candice, would say the 'mato or the 'umber. I so loved this early talk that I waited until the day she went to school before telling her not to say 'lellow' for yellow. It was a sad day.)

Toddlers are still learning to project consequences

Toddlers don't reason like adults and can't project consequences. They might not even remember fully what happened in the same situation when they pulled the table cloth, or slid on a mat a few days ago. So it's really important to be patient. We can't expect rational or even consistent behaviour. Mr 'never mind' from three paragraphs above, might demonstrate different behaviour when you try and tear him away from *Bluey,* his favourite cartoon dog, on the TV to have his bath.

More and more they see themselves as someone and something separate from others. And if they learn to do something for themselves they will fiercely demand their right to do it! When they learn what they like, they want to have it. Now! The behaviour varies from being very clingy and dependent to wanting to do EVERYTHING for themselves. You might have been subject to that great saying, 'You're not the boss of me!'

Yes, these are the 'terrible twos'. And toddlers can be very difficult. But their behaviours might relate to us having expectations, or beliefs, about them demonstrating purposeful misbehaviour, when in fact they are pretty much acting out their feelings and still consolidating how the world works.

Supporting communication

There are some things we can do to make our communication more efficient and elicit preferred behaviour.

Talk about and demonstrate feelings and emotions

It is hardly worthwhile asking a toddler, 'How do you think you made mummy feel?'.

Honestly, they have no idea. You need to point out the physical manifestations of feelings to them when the opportunities present themselves. In the park you say, 'See the little girl crying. She is sad because her ice cream fell on the ground.' At home you might say, 'Daddy is smiling. He is happy because we are all ready to hop in the car to visit Uncle Ron' or 'Mummy jumped because she got a fright. She didn't expect the kitty to jump up on her lap!' In these sentences, the emotion is linked to what they child can see in the face and body of others. You can also explain their own feelings to them. 'Mattie is sad (mirroring his sad face) because Lucy has to go now. But don't worry, she'll be home later.'

When I was teaching, we had the occasional child with severe separation anxiety. It helped when I placed myself in close proximity, reassured them, acknowledged their feelings and tried to give them a picture of what would happen to change their feelings later. For one child, I had to draw the story each morning for a couple of weeks.

> *Mummy drove you to kinder in the car. You are here with us now. She is driving to work. When she is finished, she will drive to the shops to get dinner, then she'll drive back here. You will go in the car with Mummy and have dinner with everyone at home. Show me your house. Show me the car. Where is Mummy's work. Where are the shops. Is Mummy coming back to get you? Can we go and find something to do together?*

Wasn't I blessed that we always had two educators in the room so I could go through this routine? The anxiety subsided, he settled, and went to a favourite play area in the mornings.

You can also provide the children with the language to address the emotions like 'never mind'. Or 'I'm so sorry you feel sad, but soon you will feel happy again when … '. 'I know you're feeling angry now, and you are yelling. I understand. Sometimes I also feel angry. It helps if I go for a little walk to get rid of the angry energy.'

You won't escape all the tantrums, but there will be fewer if the children have things explained to them so that they start to be able to name their feelings and have some simple strategies you can enact together to overcome them.

More tune in, talk more and take turns
You read about Dana Suskind's three ways to encourage language development in the first chapter. Now you will use the tools at a more advanced level.

Tuning in between 18 months and three years means observing what is interesting to the child and adjusting your commentary to it. If we follow what the child is engaged with, following their gaze, there is evidence that the cognitive complexity and motivation accompanying the learning is greatly enhanced at this young age and also in subsequent ages. Children generally invest more in their own ideas (Stipek & Seal, 2001).

It is important to talk out loud

As children learn language, they start to understand what they hear (receptive language) before they can use the language (expressive language). In receptive language they are putting things together in chunks of understanding, not individual words. They see you cutting an apple into 16 perfectly even slices (I know you do it), and they 'know' you are preparing it for them to eat. They don't think to themselves: 'Those insanely precision-cut slices of Pink Lady apple are being artfully arranged on that over-decorated melamine plate for me.' Equally, they don't only see you, the knife, the apple, the plate and the slicing as unconnected, episodic things, they see them as connected. They understand your intention. The child actively interprets the world, connecting what they see into expectations of what might occur.

Margaret Donaldson, in her wonderful book *Children's Minds*, says that they build up a model of the world. It is a system of inner representation that helps them to anticipate events and deal with them. Children start to predict. They use what they have experienced in the past, what they see in front of them, your words, and how you say the words, to cue them in to what is going on. 'It is an active process of structuring and making sense of the whole' (Donaldson, 1984).

As children interpret your intentions, you can leave them partially in the dark to come up with their own conclusions, or you can help them to put it together by describing what you are doing out loud. For toddlers up to three years old, the emphasis should be on describing and naming the objects and events. Of course, you can also explain why you're doing things, but conversations which include the logical relationships, cause and effect and consequences will become more important from 3–7 years.

When children hear your words in the flow of action, the general global prediction and understanding of intention become more refined. They don't watch you preparing the apple and just sense 'eat'. They start to know more about each element in the process. The name of the knife and apple, how the knife is used, where it belongs in the kitchen and where we buy apples.

I often use the example of children carrying a bucket of water to and from a sandpit. The child is open to hearing about what he or she is attending to and begins to see him- or herself as having a respected role in a social dialogue.

As toddlers and three-year-olds carry buckets of water over a short distance and pour the liquid into the sandpit, they are 'understanding' what they are doing via many sensations. The way the water behaves as they move becomes apparent to them. They feel qualities of the water: weight, volume, flow, spills; or qualities of the sand: absorption, texture, porousness, etc. As they repeat the activity, they adjust their balance, develop a sense of expectation, and engage in prediction. Although the experiential learning is language free, *it can be enhanced by connecting it to language.*

When the child returns after a few trips, you might remark that they are balancing the bucket better, that they are spilling less water, that they are getting better at the task. We can ask what they expect to see. If they have the language, let them answer, if not, answer the question for them.

'What is happening to the water? Is it sinking into the sand? Does it happen every time?' Then comment: 'You know what to expect now, don't you – you've seen it happen a few times!'

They may not fully understand all the commentary, but they'll get the gist and understand that what they are doing is clearly of interest and value. It will make them more self-conscious of the task and help them begin to develop a functional receptive language in context around the activity.

Providing language within the context of the young student's activity and exploration is more effectual than providing decontextualised language.

Expand the goals of your communication

You can provide language for targeted goals. It can relate to the emotional aspect of the task or to the learning component.

To highlight emotion, tell them how carefully the task is being done, that they must be proud of their activity, that it has meaning to others.

Some informational comments might be: 'You have the bright red bucket with the white handle. I think this is the fourth time you have completed this circuit! Four times there and four times back! A lot of fun as you work hard! Did you remember using your bucket when you were on holiday at the beach last week?'

When this conversation occurs around the activity, the child is learning how words occur in language frames. They construct language componentry from responding to repeated patterns. He or she is now able to connect the experience to the world outside of the self.

They meet the world in words.

Arranging the environment

Safety first is the maxim when children are changing from infants to crawlers to toddlers to walkers, hoppers, skippers, jumpers, ladder-climbers, gate-riders and crazy mad scooter fiends!

Many people are critical of some of the locomotion and minding aids I used with my kids. Jolly jumpers, playpens, walking rings have all come under fire for different reasons over time. I agree that if you put the kids in these things for hours or days on end, it can impact their general development and wellbeing, but to get a few minutes respite and give you free hands for short periods of time makes them or similar aids very valuable.

In our house we had a play pen just so I could have a couple of minutes out of the room. I was tickled one day, when I came back and found husband, Pierre, on a small chair in the playpen and Sean outside it trying to get in. Pac Man had just come on the market. Pierre had the console and was playing it on the TV! This story gets retold at least three times a year!

Of course, all your precious valuables should be out of reach!

A range of good quality toys, puzzles and books are a great asset at this age. They facilitate language development, motor skills, spatial perception, hand-eye coordination, pattern recognition and thinking.

In our local suburbs, there's often access to toy and other libraries so that we can offer children a range of these experiences. The idea is not to leave them to play on their own, although of course they can do that for some of the time, but to use the time to imprint important concepts they'll need later when their learning becomes more formal.

Umbrella concepts in early language development
As you read a book, talk about the colours, shapes and numbers that are clearly evident on the page. Name the colours and shapes. As an added layer, use an *umbrella concept* as well as the name of the colour, shape or number when you do this. So, don't just say, 'the bucket is blue', say, 'the bucket is a blue colour. The spade is a red colour. The book is a square shape. The little bear is a small size.'

It sounds clunky, I know, and you don't have to do it every time. But when you do it, your child starts to recognise things belong in categories. Once your child can use the umbrella concepts themselves, you can stop doing it.

Why use these umbrella concepts?

As stated, umbrella concepts are category words. There is no actual 'colour' colour, or 'shape' shape. They are the category nouns for many other words. Categories are excellent for organising knowledge. When a child gets what colour is, they automatically shift all colours into a colour schema. Human beings have been using this organising system for centuries. Colours are pretty simple but imagine when you start talking about different kinds of 'weather'. The child learns that rain is weather, mist is weather, fog, snow, mizzle, drizzle, thunderstorms are all weather. They are more able to understand the similarities and differences between them because they all relate to how water changes in different weather conditions. So, providing early umbrella concepts set children up for using them in more complex ways later.

Activities, outings and practical ideas

Matching and sorting

Even at this very early age, you can start to set your children up with important mathematical knowledge. Count out the pieces as you arrange a four- or six-piece puzzle for them to complete on the floor. Alert them to why the pieces fit together because the colours match, or the pieces complete a face.

Ask them to put all the red blocks together. Alert them to sorting by shape colour and size.

Count out low numbers of objects. It is better for children to match an object to a number and realise that the numbers are referring to an increase in the number of objects than it is for them to learn to count to 10 or 20 with no reference to the conceptual meaning of what a number is. Yes, they do need to know the order of the numbers, but saying the numbers doesn't mean children have an understanding of numbers.

When they play at the Tupperware cupboard now, get them to sort the lids, bowls and other paraphernalia by size, colour and shape and do some simple counting. But please make it fun. Don't make it a chore.

Water and sand play
Children cannot get enough of water and sand play. This can be provided indoors as well as outdoors.

Indoors put the child in a blow-up plastic swimming pool. (Watch the ALDI catalogue! It'll probably include the foot pump!) Put a plastic dish of water in the pool with different sized containers, straws, tubes and funnels. The same can be done with sand.

The children learn about volume, texture and a multitude of other science and maths ideas while they are playing and you can help them learn them if you say words like full, empty, half-full, pour quickly, pour slowly, heavy, light, more, less, three scoops, put it in the bigger bowl ...

I am sure you get the idea of how valuable this early play can be.

Going from receptive to expressive language
The child may still not say any of these words. They receive and store them in receptive language. When they learn to say the words, it will seem like they mastered two hundred words overnight. But they've been depositing them in their word banks for ages before they use them.

In my own family, the story goes that my younger sister, Helene, didn't utter a word until she was two and a half years old. Then she spent an Easter weekend with our Aunty Joy and came home speaking non-stop in full sentences. What we realised was that she didn't need to say anything before that, because I said everything for her (Miss bossy boots). But when she had no spokesperson, translator and interpreter, she had to do it for herself. And she hasn't stopped talking since!

Round and about
Taking toddlers out of the home is a mixed joy. You love showing them off, and you have chores to do, but they can be very demanding and disgruntled out of their home environment. They might also become wary of strangers.

Being active in the outdoors is highly desirable. Children's gross motor abilities develop before their fine motor ones. So, using their bodies, arms, legs and trunks to walk, run, hop, jump, roll and climb is an excellent basis for later schoolwork. Besides this they just love the sheer feel of being active. If you want to, you can create some fun exercises where they 'cross the midline'. That is, they touch their toes or reach across in some way that a right part of their body is in contact with another part on the opposite side. This midline crossing encourages communication across the whole brain and is very stimulating to learning.

You can help children feel settled and cooperative by having something familiar with them. (I am sure you know people who still have the much-loved ear-torn teddy on a shelf somewhere?) Bring the sense of security and the routine with you. Bring a small container of a snack they like, a book they particularly love to 'read', or a small activity to keep them occupied. These days, of course there is the digital revolution! The phone or iPad can be a godsend. There are some fabulous games and apps for this young set, the generation that was born into the digital revolution.

I briefly mentioned the danger of device addiction in the introduction, but the digital age is here to stay, so supervised, balanced use of digital devices can also add to children's literacy. But don't forget the books. It is amusing to see toddlers spreading their fingers across a picture in a book to expand its size, but that in itself is a warning not to forget all the different modes of literacy.

Expression through art and movement

Loris Malaguzzi was the progenitor of the Reggio Emilia philosophy I mentioned in the opening paragraphs of this book. One of his most profound legacies, is our understanding that children do not have one or two, but 100 languages for expressing themselves.

> The child
>
> is made of one hundred.
>
> The child has a hundred languages
>
> a hundred hands
>
> a hundred thoughts
>
> a hundred ways of thinking ...

This excerpt from Malaguzzi's poem emphasises the multi-modal nature of communication.

Communication is internal, in the mind and the emotions; and external, expressed with the voice and the body. It is the infinite ways to manipulate and use materials. The educators in Reggio Emilia talk about 'the expressive, the communicative and the cognitive languages' (Editors, Edwards, Gandini, & Foreman, 1998).

Hearts and Sun, Miranda, 4 years

Children use drawing, painting, movement, gesture, singing, rhythm, vocalisation, construction, dance and many other means of expressing themselves. Offering children materials for visual and movement arts in the first years of life gives them valuable ways to express themselves.

We have already mentioned the interest factor of the cardboard box. Early art doesn't have to be complex; it should be investigative and experimental. Drawing and painting can be offered. But simply providing a variety of paper of different thicknesses, textures and sizes to crawl over, tear, crumple, cover your face or drag along with you are enough to engage and entertain children.

Suffice it to say, that toddlers and very young children up to the age of three are active, adventurous, reliant, independent, mobile, moody and marvellous fun to be with.

IN SUMMARY:

- According to Piaget's developmental stages, toddlers and young children between 18 months and three years are crossing over from the sensorimotor to the preoperational stage
- They are actively learning language although it is more receptive than expressive
- They understand a cluster of events to interpret the intentions of others around them
- They use symbols like words and understand pictures, but they don't yet have the ability for complex logical reasoning and may not fully understand even the words they are using
- They are described as egocentric because their chief concern is themselves and their immediate environment
- This egocentricity is not 'selfish', but rather is related to the fact that they are still learning how the world works
- They benefit from a secure but also stimulating environment
- Their language development relies on what they can physically see in the here and now and they are more able to absorb language if it relates to what they are doing. It helps for adults to 'share their gaze'
- Very early concepts like colour, shape, size and simple numbers can be included in their day-to-day play
- It is useful to add the umbrella concepts to adjectives like blue *colour*, round shape and small *size* to their vocabulary
- Talking out loud explaining what you are doing helps toddlers to develop logical connections between objects and actions.

Preschoolers

CHAPTER THREE

Emerging from the Chrysalis Preschool (3 to 5 years)

'All people – and I mean scholars, researchers and teachers who in any place have set themselves to study children seriously – have ended up by discovering not so much the limits and weaknesses of children but rather their surprising and extraordinary strengths and capabilities linked with an inexhaustible need for expression and realisation.'
Loris Malaguzzi

Butterfly emerging from chrysalis

There is a story about a gardener who happened on a butterfly emerging from its chrysalis. Fascinated he stood and watched. At some point, the butterfly stopped its efforts. Thinking the butterfly had run out of energy, the gardener gently cut the tip of the chrysalis with his sheers to give it easy release. The butterfly emerged and plopped down to the grassy patch below. But its body was bulgy and fat and its wings were stumpy and small. The gardener waited for the wings to stretch out and the butterfly to take off … but it never did. Truncating the butterfly's struggle, had in effect prevented the final stage of metamorphosis where the liquid from the bulgy body, was pushed into the stumpy wings. The butterfly's struggle is part of its transformation.

The preschool years are a truly amazing stage of a child's life metamorphosis and we can either help it or hamper it.

It takes as long as it takes
Have you ever got yourself entangled in a doona cover that just won't go onto the doona! And then there are the blasted buttons, ten of them. They're so inconvenient and the buttonholes are too small for the buttons! Changing the bedcovers used to just leave me in a seriously bad mood. One day, I said to myself 'Lil, it takes as long as it takes'. Immediately I relaxed. It was such a relief to just give in to the idea. Not everything can happen when you want it in the time you want it.

And children are much more important than doona covers!

As a director of early learning at a school in Melbourne, I saw 132 different families enter the premises over a week. Families turned up in their infinite variety with different family dynamics.

For starters, each child was lucky because they were being dropped off in the first place! They were being afforded the opportunity to venture beyond their homes to play and learn with caring educators and peers. Many children the world over don't have this privilege.

Some parents arrived with what I called the pram pantechnicon. (I love the word *pantechnicon* because it was my son Sean's favourite word as a three-year-old, when he learned that it was the 'real' word for his much-loved double trailer toy trucks he used to call 'pampelas'.) The pantechnicon pram had two seats, one in front of the other, for infants and toddlers, and a step at the back for a third child to stand between the parent's arms as the whole balagan raced into the central concourse called the *piazza*. (I might be accused of cultural appropriation, but I love the Jewish word *balagan* for chaos or fiasco.) I knew that not one child had taken one step from the moment they got out of bed until the moment they were lifted from the pram at kinder. That included the five-year old standing on the back!

Believe me, I have total sympathy for any parent who could juggle all this in a morning. But not even the five-year-old had actually dressed herself or walked to the car! Most children were in strollers or prams way beyond where they were capable of walking for themselves. I would have been less concerned if this only happened in the morning when everyone was running late, but in most cases the kids were also bundled up and wheeled off at speed after kinder.

Not walking for yourself, not being able to adjust your own pace, not having the ability to do a little exploration and pick up a stone, run a stick along a paling fence to hear the rat-a-tat sound. Not being in control impacts on competence and a sense of independence.

I don't want you to think I am being critical of the parents in this rushed scenario. Our world is so fast- paced that they are just doing what they can to cope. But a fast-paced world is out of kilter with a slow-paced child. One of the greatest gifts we can give children is time. Time to explore at their own pace.

Footprints in snow

There is a great story about the famous architect Frank Lloyd Wright who on a morning when he was a boy walked across a field of snow with his no-nonsense uncle. When they got to the end of the field, the uncle said to him, 'See how your tracks wander all over the place from the fence to the woods and everywhere? Now look at my tracks. They come straight across the field directly to the goal. There is a lesson here about staying on track!'

With a twinkle in his eye Frank reflects how that experience was formative in his life because he took the exact opposite of his uncle's advice and 'determined right then, not to miss most things in life, as my uncle had' (Shelby church, 2021).

This story is about having patience for your child to explore. Time to move, turn their attention from one thing to another, see, feel, hear, taste and become more themselves. Children need time.

My wish is that the same hurried children marshalled into kinder in the morning experienced more leisurely experiences in the evenings and at weekends where they could acquire independence. Independence is the keyword for kindergarten. There is a popular maxim, 'don't do anything for a child they can do for themselves'. My only rider to this is, that like us, there are times when a child is so frazzled and emotionally stuck, that even if they know how, you doing it for them on that occasion will be a godsend.

Supporting preschoolers
From three to five years of age, children are developing so rapidly in so many ways that it's hard to keep up! Language, physical growth, locomotion, socialisation, emotional awareness, cognition and thinking are all racing forward.

Some children are incredibly lucky and these domains progress together and balance each other out so they feel in harmony with themselves. They have a sense of equilibrium.

But for most children, some of these developmental areas move forward at a faster pace than others.

I think we all know a child who shot up to be as tall as peers two years older. With this comes a raft of expectations for which he or she isn't ready. They might be judged harshly for behaviours that are age appropriate, but which they 'look' too old to present with.

Some children are ahead in their learning, so they can recite the alphabet, count to a hundred, perhaps even read; but the minute something doesn't go their way, they morph into a raging, roiling tantrum that it is almost impossible to deal with!

Some children have a wonderful creative idea they want to enact at the painting easel, but their hand-eye coordination isn't up to the task and they suddenly paint over all their work in frustration.

When we understand that different aspects of development go at different paces, we are more able to support our children through this stage and enjoy the incredible wonder of how quickly they are gaining new knowledge and skills. We can also view each of our children as having their own mould, their own timing and their own disposition.

Focal area of development

Preschool is where the metamorphosis from infant to school goer happens.

As a preschool specialist I often smiled to myself when I heard parents say that the first year of formal schooling was when their children blossomed and learnt more than any other year! It is true that the foundation or prep year of formal school is like that. But the idea that it is so important is often based on the fact that children learn to read and write in prep. It is easy to see and monitor these giant early literacy achievements. But reading and writing, as you will see further down, are the very tip of the iceberg! What happens at preschool, and even before that, is the immense preliminary learning journey that underpins reading and writing.

Preschooler as thinker and learner
If I return to Piaget for a minute, we said that the age two to seven was the preoperational stage and that the children weren't capable of complex logic. I was happy to say that for children aged two or three, but between three and six, I and other educators and theorists are not in complete agreement with Piaget's assessment.

Piaget's assessments were often based on experiments where young children couldn't understand something called 'conservation of constancy'. For example, if you take a small jug of water filled to the brim and pour it into a larger jug and ask a child if there is more or less water in the big jug, they'll often say less, because that is what they see. Also, if you take a ball of plasticine and roll it out into a flat pizza-like circle and ask them if there is more or less plasticine, they will say there is more, because it appears bigger to them. The *constancy*, that it is indeed the same amount, obviously exists, but children's senses can't validate it.

What we have realised is that conservation of constancy is by far not the only measure of logic! Some children are remarkable in their ability to reason things out. A mum of a four-year-old, Miranda, told me a story one morning. She was pouring milk for Miranda and her two-year-old brother, James. Because James was about to have his dinner, she poured out half a glass for him and a full tumbler for his sister. James set about crying and yelling in protest. The mum tried to reason with him. In the meantime, Miranda went to the cupboard, returned with a tumbler half the size and poured the half drink into the small tumbler which filled it up! James shut up like a clam, sighed a big shuddering sigh, took the tumbler and drank the milk without another peep.

Take a minute to think about what a four-year-old child had done in logical terms with this small act of genius. She has assessed that it wasn't the amount that had got her brother upset, but that the glass was half full. Pretty much he felt it was unfair. Then she went through a problem-solving exercise and acted on it. I was honestly amazed by the complex logic in the solution. She has demonstrated fully her understanding of the conservation of constancy, but it meant something in the context. Besides the good thinking in there, she displayed genuine empathy in her desire and action to make James feel better about life ... and his milk.

In context, when things are going on around children and we are doing tasks and using objects, young children defy the traditional beliefs and present with incredible logic. And we can help them to do this simply by talking out loud!

Supporting communication

Think and link aloud
It is hard to divide learning up into literacy, maths, science, arts, ethics, geography and history subjects because a lot of the time they are all happening together. I know you're interested in literacy, maths and science. But the first thing I want to say is that all of these subjects are founded on understanding language. It simply can't be stressed enough. So, language first, and subjects later.

Words, words, words!
What do you think of when I say that words are important? It is common to think of words as names for objects. Apple, TV, shoe, dog, harpsicord, rainbow, combustion engine. As you read the list, you will have had a sense of each belonging to different categories, because there are no clear connections between them. They are random.

Children do learn the names for an inordinate number of things, but when I talk about language, I want you to see it as a much more connected and cohesive thing. When we focus on early learning of any subject, a really important thing to know is that everything occurs in relationship to other things. Nothing learned in isolation has much value.

When you think and link out loud (I almost made this phrase the title of this book it is so important) you will provide your child with the important logical and relational connections between things around them. Language is how words, words, words connect ideas.

A very simple example I give is about changing your mind. You might say to a three-year-old, 'We aren't going to the shops anymore, so you can go and do some drawing'. Or you might say, 'Uh-oh, I planned for us to go to the supermarket to get dinner things, but it has started to rain very hard outside. Come and have a look. If we go right now, we're going to get soaking wet. I've changed my mind, let's plan to go a little later when the rain has passed. So, you have time to do some drawing now. Do you think that's a good plan?'.

In the second communication, and it hardly takes more time to say, you are including your child in the logical explanation of the change. They see the connection between the weather and the delay. You are also providing language that describes mental processes like think, plan, change your mind. Finally, there is a respectful inclusiveness about your statement. The decision includes them and isn't made outside of them.

Before we get to subject areas like literacy, maths and science, let's look at knowledge in general. Over the years I have distilled knowledge into four words: know, connect, mobilise, communicate.

Know
We've discussed infancy in some detail, so you've seen how children commence knowing things from birth and possibly even before that when they respond to stimuli in the womb. The information enters their body and brain through sensory pathways.

Over time, they start to recognise sequences of events and patterns around them. They hear footsteps in the corridor and know you are on your way. They can distinguish their immediate caregivers from other people, they start to recognise objects and anticipate events. Understanding what is happening around them adds meaning to what they are sensing and they develop perception. Perception is experience that is elevated from a sensory experience because it is interpreted into meaning for the child. They don't only 'feel' something they 'know' something.

As they grow and develop in the immediate family and community, they hear words and labels for what they see, feel and know. Initially their language might be quite unique, they might call the cat 'boo', and their grandma, 'lala'. Sometimes, as in my family, that grandma becomes 'Lala' for life!

But eventually children learn the labels for all the persons, objects and events in their everyday lives.

Initially, they might only think about what they can see and perceive in the here and now, but soon they are able to *visualise* what they know. This is a quantum leap in knowing. When children carry these visualisations and knowledge around in their minds, they have developed conceptual language which is crucial for all later learning. When they have conceptual understanding, they can apply their knowledge more broadly. They might realise that their friends also go to the shops to buy groceries and have a grandma, even though her name might be γιαγιά!

Parents will spend a huge amount of time giving their children the names and labels for things. Spend a day with a toddler who points at something and then looks at you quizzically? His face says, what's the name for this? Children's curiosity and desire to know is legendary! I think Rudyard Kipling had it perfectly correct in his poem:

From the second she opens her eyes
One million Hows, Two million Wheres,
And seven million Whys!
Rudyard Kipling – The Elephant's Child

But labels, whilst valuable, are simply not enough. Children need to learn why Lala is a grandma, and what the groceries are used for. So, the second kind of knowledge you want to develop is the ability to connect.

Connect
How do you get your child to connect knowledge? I think the most logical way is to think about whole and parts. Let's take a cup. Ask your child about the parts and the functions of the parts. Even kindergarten children will be able to explain that a cup needs a bottom and sides to hold the liquid, that it needs a handle to protect your hand from heat and that the rim needs to be smooth, so you don't hurt your mouth when you drink. These are what I call *internal connections*. They seem so simple, but they are crucial to conceptual understanding. And internal connections exist in everything from the cup to an electromagnet. If children start early to see and elaborate these internal connections, they are setting up their brains to see them everywhere. They get a superhighway for connecting stuff!

Once the internal connections are established, we can focus on *external connections*. And there are several ways to make external connections.

External connections to similar items
Let's start with comparing the mug to other crockery. How is a cup the same and different from a saucer, plate, bowl, or cake stand? What are the distinctive features and function of each and how does the design facilitate the function?

What you are encouraging your child to do when they consider things in this way is *to compare*. If you ask me as an educator what is the most important thinking skill to embed in students, I will definitively say 'comparison'. Comparison brings order and organisation to our thinking. Nothing exists on its own. Everything exists in relationship to other things. Each thing has its own features, and the features are either exactly the same, similar or different to those features in other things.

If your child has mastered the art of distinguishing the features of something, and the skill of comparing, they are set up to solve almost any task, or problem that comes their way. Encourage them to compare their dolls, cars, clothes, pets, breakfast, feelings and everything else under the sun. The minute you get them to compare their vocabulary will explode! One doll is small, another is big. One toy vehicle is yellow and a taxi, another is blue and pantechnicon. One sweater is soft and silky, another is rough and scratchy.

External connections that are not immediately evident
I don't think we have any idea how many connections between things are invisible to children. Indeed, I think the majority of our understanding is based on things we 'know' rather than connections we can 'see'. We have to help children to 'project virtual relationships' between things. The cup from before is a perfect example.

The cup provides a means of positive socialisation. It facilitates the global offering of hospitality. When a friend comes around, one of the first things you do is offer them a drink. For good friends it may be a velvety glass of red wine, for a neighbour, an afternoon cuppa, for children, milk, water or cordial. The cup is a symbol of friendship.

Not all connections are immediately evident to the child, or even to us. The connection of the cup to friendship is 'invisible' to the child. Your preschooler might automatically make the connection and offer their friends a drink, but not all children pick up these abstract clues so easily.

This is where thinking and linking out loud becomes extremely important. You are the communicator of words, but more importantly the communicator of connections. You uncover the features for comparison and logical relationships.

As you set out a tray, with the beautiful, embroidered cloth you inherited from your grandmother, you say, 'Uncle George and Auntie Mary are coming over today. I'm setting the tray for afternoon tea. It's so nice to give your visitors something to eat and drink. It makes them feel welcome and special. I know Uncle George just loves my jam scones so that's why I had you help me make them this morning. What do you think you should give Emma when she comes over for a play date tomorrow?'

As with the cup, you can ask your child to expand on the 'why' behind a multitude of items and events. If you think they might know the answer, ask questions. When you reach the outer limit of their knowledge, provide information. Provide the necessary links.

A further type of external connection I have already mentioned, is connecting things to umbrella concepts.

External connection to umbrella concepts
When I mentioned the cup, I indicated you could compare it to what was similar, crockery. It is similar because crockery is made of china or porcelain, and it is used for eating and drinking. 'Crockery' is an umbrella concept for all these eating and drinking items. There isn't a thing called a crockery in the world. It is a word representing a group, class, assortment of other items. Because umbrella concepts gather other words and bundle them together, they help your child to organise their understanding of the relationship between things.

You have already encountered the idea earlier in the book, but here you can see it as improving a child's ability to understand things more clearly and organise their thinking. So as often as you can, use a category word. Ask them to: 'Get the fork from the *cutlery* drawer', 'Find the screwdriver in the *tool*box.' Say, 'I wonder if it's going to rain, let's check the *weather* report.' Ask, 'Which kind of *transport* shall we use today, train, car or tram?'

These statements, requests and questions constantly organise individual words into groups. When your child is asked to write an essay on pollution, they won't be flummoxed, they'll list the types: water, air, plastic, soil, noise and perhaps even radioactive and then get to work writing the essay. (No, I don't expect your preschooler to do that of course, but I do want you to give them hundreds of category words so when they encounter these tasks, they have the concepts and the vocabulary to smash them out.)

Connecting information in the ways above is excellent and you can see how your child will have a deeper knowledge of everything. But you want to go even further. You want them to use the knowledge to achieve something. You want them to solve a problem, carry out a plan, enact a solution or even create something new. You want them to mobilise their knowledge. When children use their own knowledge to solve problems and make plans, they have an exponential escalation in their independence.

Mobilise

The third kind of knowledge goes beyond knowing and connecting. Your child might know the difference between a screwdriver and a hammer, but the information is only valuable when they actually use the knowledge for an outcome. You will know they have it when you're ruining a knife from your cutlery set trying to change an electric plug, and daughter number two turns up beside you, dressed as a pirate, with the Phillips head screwdriver.

As much as possible, give your children opportunities to use their knowledge.

As an early learning director, I was regularly amused, amazed and sometimes horrified when a child turned up at kinder in the most inappropriate clothing. A parent would lift his or her eyebrows and smile saying, Maryanne chose her outfit today. (She is resplendent in her dance leotard, no tights and the ever-popular tutu. It's 4 degrees outside.)

I am the first one to say that children need to make decisions and have choices, but there would be ways to scaffold the child to make decisions that would have a better outcome.

If the child makes the leotard-tutu choice, ask her (or him) why they wanted to wear it? It might be the colour, the association with something enjoyable or just because it's brand new. Do you leave them in a situation where they'll freeze their butt off or not be allowed outdoors that day; or do you get them thinking and problem solving?

Perhaps accept stage one; but then ask them to look out the window and assess the weather. Ask them to match the weather with something in their cupboard. The objective is for them to come up with a solution to the mismatch between their choice and the circumstances in the environment. They might decide to wear an overcoat and trousers to get to kinder and then put those in the locker when they arrive before pirouetting into the kinder room. They might decide to wear their ski outfit. In this scenario, you are encouraging them to make assessments, use their knowledge of warm and cold, appropriate and inappropriate, and come up with a solution. You are asking them to think logically and not stop at the first choice.

(You will, of course, get the prima donna whose mind refuses to change, but in that case, please bring the extra layer in the bag!) Using knowledge is a way to encourage independence and that is the key thing to develop in the preschool years.

A further way to support your children to succeed at many levels is to nurture their ability to communicate. I have a strong belief that communication is a specific kind of knowledge.

Communicate
To some it might seem strange to list communication as one of four separate headings about knowledge. But it is a unique kind of knowledge. It is the means to formulate (encode) and understand (decode) information. Your goal is for your children to express what they have learned and what they know, think, feel and imagine.

Communication can be broadly categorised into two types, verbal and non-verbal. Verbal communication includes talking, reading and writing. Non-verbal communication includes all body language and gesture, and the expression of ideas through art, music, movement and materials.

Each type of communication has its own structure, alphabet and vocabulary. Simply put, for music it is the composition, the melody and the notes. For dance it is the form, the choreography and the steps. Whether it is spoken language, painting, movement, sculpture, music or dance, there are central conventions and elements we learn to recognise to understand what is being communicated.

I have already introduced Loris Malaguzzi, the originator of the internationally renowned educational philosophy from Reggio Emilia in northern Italy, who saw children as having a hundred languages for expressing themselves. He emphasised the incredible variety of children's communication. Communication is internal, in the mind and the emotions; and external, expressed with the voice and the body. It emphasises the infinite ability of the human mind and body to create forms of expression that enable us to formulate and share our experience and our understanding of the world.

I don't think parents automatically know the real significance of all this communication.

These expressive languages should not be thought of as belonging to the curriculum area of art. Rather, this expression, using media, tools and materials, is the child's vehicle for engaging with the world to develop understanding of what it is and how it works.

As parents you will most likely highly value students' literacy as verbal communication (speaking, reading and writing). But children can become literate in all modes of communication. As human beings, there is great diversity in the modes we use to communicate information and meaning: concrete manipulative, photographic, pictorial, graphic, tabular, schematic, symbolic, verbal written, verbal spoken, gestural, postural, locomotor and digital.

Children thrive when they learn to decode and encode the structure and elements of each.

The danger of misguided literacy expectation in the preschool years
It is worth pausing here for a moment and look at parent expectations around reading and writing.

There is an ongoing debate about whether parents should be teaching their preschoolers literacy before they go to school. Parents' concern with this issue relates to their desire that their children will succeed at school.

I believe this is a debate to be conducted at a deeper level. The debate should not be about how best to teach literacy but about what actually constitutes literacy.

The most common definition of literacy is the ability to read and write. At preschool level this is, in many ways, a misguided expectation. There are several reasons for this, but the most important is that reading and writing are extremely complex cognitive and motor operations that are based on hundreds of underlying skills.

To write a single letter of the alphabet accurately onto a page, a child must have consolidated a conceptual understanding of spatial relationships. What is top, bottom, sideways, left, right, middle, curvy, straight, round, long, short, upside down and right way up. The child needs the coordination to plan the cognitive motor operations before even employing the muscular, fine-motor control to create the letter 'a'. Besides this, there is the comprehension that the 'a' is a symbolic representation of a sound made by the voice, that it is part of a word that is part of a sentence …

Reading and writing are the tiny part of the literacy iceberg that is visible above the waterline. The skills that underpin reading and writing are the hidden mass we cannot see. At preschool, some children's skills reach the level required to read and write ... *but the majority do not.*

There is a clear and hidden danger in trying to force children to acquire reading and writing skills too early. They might build up negative associations and poor self-image of themselves as learners if they're not successful. This negative experience shows up later and is very difficult to remediate. So, my heartfelt request is to focus on what your child can do successfully to learn and communicate their knowledge rather than try to force them to read and write too early. In Scandinavian countries, with the highest educational success, children only start to read and write when they are seven.

This important understanding of multiple ways of communicating ideas should be at the heart of the literacy debate. A limited definition of literacy doesn't recognise the amazing ability of children to communicate what they know, think believe and create; and we're at fault when we don't recognise this. We judge children negatively because we are accepting only the verbal modality of expression. When the concept of literacy is broadened, we recognise how children *do communicate* rather than how *they do not.*

What would a program look like if we took into account all children's ways of communicating?

Children would be moving, investigating, experimenting, planning, imagining, designing, listening, speaking and using a variety of art media. You can be doing all this in your kitchen at home! And later in the chapter I will offer my top 10 activities for children from three to five years old.

Receptive and expressive modes of communication
In general, decoding of information is arrived at first. Young children's language learning is exponential. Most often, their receptive language is

much stronger than their expressive language. It is important to scaffold and strengthen the progress from receptive to expressive language. We have already explored some ways of doing this. It takes a child about 40 repetitions of a word in context before they have genuinely consolidated it. So, even with older students, we need to be aware of developing solid vocabulary, that ensures children not only understand a word but can activate and articulate it with the appropriate meaning in the correct context.

There is a big divide between receptive understanding and auto-expression of that understanding. Expressive language doesn't only operate in conversation with others, but is also a steppingstone to children's self-talk, or what we call interior dialogue. Self-talk is a vital component in thinking and learning. Where do you do most of your thinking, planning and problem-solving? (And I'm not talking about in the car or in the shower!) When children start to internalise their thinking, and have an interior dialogue, they are well on their way to developing good problem-solving and creative skills. Your thinking and linking out loud, and your appreciation of all their modes of communication will enhance their ability to think constructively for themselves

Arranging the environment

The Reggio Emilia philosophy sees early education as a triangular partnership between the child, the family and the educators. Parents entrust their children to the day care, preschool or school environment each day in the hopes that their safety and education will be honoured and upheld. Clearly educators take their role seriously, but when your children get to kindergarten, they will be one of anything between six and 32 children.

As primary educators you have a much greater vested interested and will have a much greater impact on your child's success than they will get outside your ambit.

Before I was a parent, I had the joy of spending my well-earned weekend wages earned in a local Wimpy Hamburger outlet in Johannesburg to accompany my now husband, Pierre, to Italy on a skiing holiday. It was done on one of those bucket flight student fares. And it felt like a bucket.

On our way to Italy, we visited friends in Zurich. I was shellshocked by how the entire house was arranged for their kids! My own childhood home had spaces for children, but I had never seen a home where the kitchen, living room, bedrooms, bathrooms and even the entrance and passageways were arranged to accommodate children. There were hooks for coats at kid height as you arrived through the door. As the mum cooked, three children busied themselves drawing, cutting, pasting and colouring at a kid-sized table under a window. They had a cupboard full of stationery and art materials of different kinds.

The living room had furniture to accommodate children and there were baskets of toys and comfortable mats to sit and lie on. In those days, there were no digital devices, but there was a place for kids to watch TV close to the parents although piles of books seemed to dominate more than videos.

The house could not be called pristine or tidy and my own mother might have had a cardiac arrest to see it, but the kids were very busy, communicative, social and accomplished.

I am not suggesting that you should rearrange your entire home to suit your motley brood. My own home was never completely adapted to children. But it was a wonderful lesson to me of a lifestyle that accommodated children rather than experiencing them as a messy disturbance in life.

Run, jump, swing and slide
When we think of the environment for children aged three to five years old, one of the most important things to consider is their physical

development. In a book about language and communication, you might think this an unusual place to start.

In my private practice as a trainer in Feuerstein thinking skills, I saw children who had great difficulty with motor planning and letter formation. Motor planning is the coordination of movement and it is initiated in the brain. A child with writing difficulties, may not have the perceptual motor ability to plan the shape of letters on the page. The movements controlling writing are called fine motor skills.

The way motor skills develop is from the trunk outwards through the limbs and then to the hands, feet, fingers and toes. Fine motor skills are based on and build on good core and gross motor skills.

I found that on many occasions, the children with poor coordination hadn't developed their gross motor skills. They couldn't hop on one leg, skip or jump on two legs. Doing these exercises takes skill and involves both sides of the brain. When movement uses both sides of the brain the children become used to crossing the midline, that is, the right side of their body, is comfortable moving across into the spatial area of their left side. Think of touching opposite toes, touching opposite heels behind the body, touching opposite elbow to knee, etc.

You can check if your child's movement is developing well when you watch how they walk and run. Their right arm should come forward as they step off with their left and the gait should be smooth and rhythmic.

Crossing over and strengthening the core and limbs occurs naturally when children climb on equipment, ride bicycles, swing, play on seesaws, play hopscotch and swim. The more exercise the children do, the better their musculoskeletal system will develop and the more coordinated they'll be. Besides the strength and benefits to coordination, this also improves posture, and posture is extremely important because it triggers how others relate to your child.

Exercise can be arranged indoors during inclement weather if you design an obstacle course for them to negotiate. Kids love nothing more than diving over the back of the couch with your permission.

Activities, outings and practical ideas

Who doesn't love a good story?
As children, my siblings and I loved visiting our paternal grandmother's house. She had a glass cabinet arranged with porcelain tea sets and knick-knacks. But the real treasure was on the bottom shelf. She had a collection of hard and soft covered children's books. I think they'd passed through several generations and weren't in the greatest shape, but we were only allowed to read them if we used the utmost care. I think that was when I learnt my respect for books. *Beano, A Book of Knowledge*, a huge hard cover nursery rhyme book, a collection of Hans Christian Anderson fairy tales … it was heaven.

Listening to and reading stories is important for many reasons. Stories:

- nurture the imagination
- grow vocabulary
- teach language and story structure
- introduce inferential language
- call for interpretation of pictures
- require the evaluation and judgement of characters
- present different points of view.

To follow a story children must monitor and remember the order of events as the plot unfolds.

My daughter, Candice, learned to read at a much more complex level overnight out of sheer frustration. She was perhaps eight years old when J.K Rowling's *Harry Potter and the Philosopher's Stone* so captured her imagination that she had no capacity to wait for me or Pierre to read to her and decided to do it for herself. She never looked back and is still a prolific reader.

Between three and six, children benefit most from reading when they are doing it with you. You become the sounding board and the one who can explore and explain with them.

My advice is to always read a picture book through without interruption the first time unless they ask you a question. Then, on the second and multiple reads, you can stop and ask questions, point out the words and the letters. Ask them to tell you what happens next, ask them their opinions. Highlighting reading conventions like reading from left to right, that time is not always chronological, that stories usually have a beginning, middle and end, makes them a highly skilled reader. It is impossible to overestimate the positive effect of good reading comprehension in life and in learning. There is hardly a way to make your child into a better reader than by reading to and with them regularly if not every single day.

Almost everything that applies to reading, applies to film. But it is especially important that at least for the first time, you watch the films with your children. Some films we think are funny or harmless, may include something in them to trigger anxiety, fear or worry in your child. Because the figures move and are more lifelike, this could have long lasting effects. I am still haunted by an apocalyptic film I saw as a child called *The Omega Man*!

Colour, cut and paste
Paint, draw, cut, paste, model, mould, build. I alluded earlier to how many skills underpin reading and writing. When children are involved in arts and crafts, they aren't just making something for you to put on the fridge for a week and then turf out surreptitiously. They are developing early literacy.

These activities are doing good on several levels. Firstly, they are exercising the fine-motor muscles we discussed earlier, so crucial for writing and typing, etc. Secondly, they are building a sense of competence. As children create and produce, they are gaining a sense of themselves as producers and achievers capable of finishing projects and tasks. I intimated before that part of self-actualisation is self-mastery.

Thirdly, they are developing thinking skills. This is often an underestimated aspect of creation. To do the drawing, make the puppet, cut the paper, model the plasticine children are working towards a goal, developing a plan, sequencing their tasks, evaluating their progress, fixing errors, extending their plan in new directions and developing a sense of flow and heightened attention.

Artistic expression is thinking practice for young children. It is the kind of project and brain activity I love to encourage in the kinder room.

Rather than tell a preschooler what you see as they work, ask them what they are making?

I had the experience of suggesting to a child that she had drawn a serpent, but discovered she was drawing a water slide. They know what they're doing. And you'll be amazed by the intricacy of what they say once they start telling you!

Having a small 'studio' space for children is a great invitation to get busy. And it is important that they work with you for the clean-up. They should start from an early age to understand that what you mess up you clean up.

Games, puzzles and construction

Playing board games and cards with your children has fantastic outcomes. A primary advantage is they exercise self-regulation. They learn, not all at the same pace or as easily, that you can't win all the time, you oughtn't cheat and it's important to be a good sport and lose with grace. But besides all those great social skills these games develop strategic planning and thinking.

Puzzles likewise sharpen maths skills like matching, sorting, comparing, planning and hypothetical (if … then) thinking, for example, 'If this piece has green on it, then it could be part of the hat.'

Construction toys can keep children involved for hours. Unlike a teddy or Barbie, which might be one dimensional toys, construction is open-ended, grows in stages, develops coordination and encourages planning and problem solving. I couldn't count the hours my children spent playing with blocks, Duplo, Lego, Lasy, and other kinds of construction toys. This play also enhances attention, extends perseverance and teaches children to deal with frustration.

As with reading, watching films and art projects, they gain infinitely more out of these fun activities if you spend time doing it with them.

Top 10 activities for children 3–5 years old
1. Reading together
2. Games that involve colour and shape recognition
3. Listening to music and dancing to the rhythm
4. Baking together
5. Designing and negotiating an obstacle course
6. Working in the garden
7. Helping to collect groceries at the supermarket
8. Watching a movie together
9. Going for exploratory family walks
10. Responsible pet care

IN SUMMARY:

- Preschool children learn at different rates and need time to explore and develop independence
- Their emotional social, physical and cognitive development might not progress at the same pace, so patience and understanding are required
- The preschool years are crucial for language development
- Children learn to understand language (receptive language) before they learn to use it (expressive language)
- Preschoolers start to develop concepts they can visualise in their minds and begin to use logical thinking
- It is valuable to offer children means of expression other than focusing on reading and writing
- Art materials, books, construction and board games are meaningful supports for their learning
- They may not see the 'invisible' links and relationships between things, so talking out loud in a way that explains these is very helpful
- Physical activity is important to develop both gross and fine motor coordination
- Understanding the body in space helps to develop motor planning for many different activities
- Beyond knowing a label for something, this is a time to connect, use and communicate ideas.

School-aged children

CHAPTER FOUR

A Shining Morning Face
Junior Primary
(5 to 9 years)

*'Then, the whining schoolboy with his satchel
And shining morning face, creeping like snail
Unwillingly to school.'*
William Shakespeare

I found my own first year of school contradictory. My teacher, Mrs O'Consky was very organised. One of her tricks to support our efforts to write was to give us each a pattern book. It was an exercise book cut precisely in half. I got a bottom half and I wasn't happy about it. I liked the broad margin at the top of a page. Her instruction was, 'Whenever you have a bit of time, draw a pattern in your book.' She carefully demonstrated on the board a pattern that flowed up and down between two wide lines. Next, tulips. A cup with three little arrow shapes in a row. You know that pattern. Finally, a spiky zig zag at perfect intervals.

My mother was a fabulous artist and I had been drawing since I could hold a pencil. One day Mrs O'Consky had a knock at the door and spent about 12 minutes chatting to someone about something. The class became a bit rowdy and she turned around a few times to hush us. I took the opportunity and dutifully filled half my pattern book. She returned to the front of the room and looked down to where I was still furiously patterning. She grabbed my hand away and said, 'You're not supposed to fill the whole thing up in one sitting. That book should last you the whole term!'

I clearly never had her sense of timing!

When your child goes to school anything can and everything will happen. Good stuff, bad stuff and everything in between. But we'll focus on *the real* stuff.

Earlier I alluded to how parents value the first year of school because that is where 'the real stuff' happens. I've also explained that a lot of 'real stuff' was happening all along. But the focus on the first year of formal schooling is definitely on reading and writing. Early literacy education is wonderful for the children who are successful at it, but it can be a nightmare for children who don't get it immediately or seem never to get it at all!

In this chapter, there is a lot to cover, so the structure is a little different. For ease of use it made more sense to discuss supporting communication, arranging the environment and activities, outings and practical ideas alongside each of the focal areas of development relating to colour, shape, size, location, reading, writing and numbers.

Focal area of development

Child connecting knowledge

Crucial language learning at school is more than acquiring new vocabulary. It's a time for mastering abstract thinking, consolidating concepts and developing conceptual understanding. Knowing an isolated concept is no longer enough, children need to understand how concepts are connected and influence one another. For example, it is limiting for a child to know that a plant needs water if they don't apply the information when they see a plant with drooping leaves. Or if they don't apply the information to all plants and agriculture of plants. Conceptual understanding is knowing what something is, being able to think about it and understand how it relates to other things. Before you get to the section on concept-based understanding, I want to interject two ideas: broadening interests and encouraging creative projects.

Broaden children's interests and encourage creative projects
A great friend of mine, Dr Kathleen Buchanan, a drama expert, mother and grandmother taught me this. To help frame an identity and be taken seriously in the classroom, children need to have an interest they can talk about. Like her adult children years ago, her grandchildren are taken to the library and allowed to browse through the shelves and select books once a week to stimulate their interests. Encouraging interests is vital. Whether your child settles on spiders, frogs, gemstones or motors, it benefits them to be an 'expert' at something. The spin-off is that once they're acknowledged for what they know, they're motivated to either go deeper into the area of interest or range further to gather more interests. Having deep and complex interests enhances self-esteem and further supports self-mastery. The more knowledge and techniques and skills your child develops, the more he or she will have to draw on when operating in the world.

Extramural activities
Expose primary school children to as many activities related to sport and the arts as you can. A trip to the theatre can have a lasting effect on children's perceptions as they unconsciously respond to emotional qualities of movement, design, character and costumes. I know that I carry impressions in my brain from many visits to the theatre as a child.

The performances were occasionally staged at a prestigious theatre, but mostly they were local pantomimes and productions put on at schools or by communities. You don't have to spend a fortune on arts events if you look out for what's happening locally.

As an adjunct to the sequential structured information below, encourage your children to embark on creative projects during which they can use everything you will read about next.

Concept-based understanding of the world

I am about to introduce four concepts that at first glance appear simple. And the section will sound quite academic. But the four concepts: colour, shape, size and position begin to introduce your children to different modes of thinking. If they acquire the concepts and modes of thinking in a structured way, it will support their literacy and maths learning.

A concept is an idea you can hold in your head and is the foundation of abstract thinking. It is not the apple you can see, but the apple you can visualise in your mind. As a parent you are in a great position to help your children develop conceptual understanding. Of course, you can leave it solely to their teachers. But I have emphasised before that you are their primary educator. If you use your proximity to them day in and day out, you can put them ahead of many of their peers in their detailed comprehension of the world around them.

Colour, shape, size and location

Let's talk about colour, shape, size and location. Once you've read all about them, I hope you'll see how foundational they are to both literacy and maths. The different kinds of thinking that will be unlocked as we explore the concepts are:

- organised thinking
- associative thinking

- abstract thinking
- analytical thinking
- perspectival thinking
- relative thinking.

Don't worry too much about these thinking modes now, they'll become clear as you follow the conceptual roadmap below.

But before we commence, I'd like to share two things:

- the first is to define your parental role as a mediator of learning, not a traditional teacher
- the second is to introduce an easy five-step LAVA TUBE process you can use for introducing new concepts.

Parent as a mediator, not teacher

Mediational support

When you introduce your child to a new idea or concept, it is important that he or she is interested and focused. As a parent, the last thing you want to do is make learning a chore or try to force it. See yourself as a mediator of learning, not a teacher. As a mediator you're readily available to help your child discover and interpret things. Also, in mediation, you are a partner in the learning, walking side by side with your child. You can go forward when he or she is comfortable, stop when the learning stops, and go back when you go too far. This sensitive and empathetic partnership, where you are in tune, is not usually available in a classroom where there is a whole group to manage.

Professor Reuven Feuerstein, a Nobel Prize nominee for his work on learning and intelligence, listed three important things about mediation (Feuerstein, Rand, Hoffman, & Miller, 1980). Intentionality and reciprocity, meaning and transcendence.

Intentionality and reciprocity
First, there should be intentionality and reciprocity. You are obviously sharing something with your child so that he or she can learn and understand it. You can be as intentional as you like, but if your child is not on board to reciprocate with interest and energy and invest in what you're doing, it's a lost cause. Choose or use a time when your child is open to exploring ideas and activities with you. They need to focus and absorb what is being attended to.

Meaning
The second aspect of mediation is that it should be 'meaningful' for your child. This is not *meaning* as in a definition of something. Your child should see the *reason or purpose* for themselves in what is being considered. This might be immediately evident to the child as when it is worth their while to complete a puzzle that will satisfy them in an immediate way. But what you are aiming for is that your child also starts to see the value of spending time learning or doing something in the present that they will only need or benefit from later. This is the art

of delaying gratification. Some children can't see the value of learning maths for instance, but they might do it more readily if they know that as they do it, they are building their brains to deal with problems and challenges in the future. Meaning or purpose provides the necessary motivation to accomplish tasks.

Transcendence
The third and final aspect of mediation is that whatever is being learned should go beyond the moment and be applicable in other contexts at other times. In mediation we help children to see how what they are learning is relevant in the world around them. It is no use them knowing what a square is, or a geranium, if they don't recognise and use the knowledge beyond their home or garden.

In a classroom environment educators may or may not be in step with your child, but you are in the position to understand where they are in their learning. If children miss out on important concepts as they progress through school it can have long-term effects on their performance and by extension, their self-confidence and esteem.

Five-step LAVA TUBE method for introducing new concepts

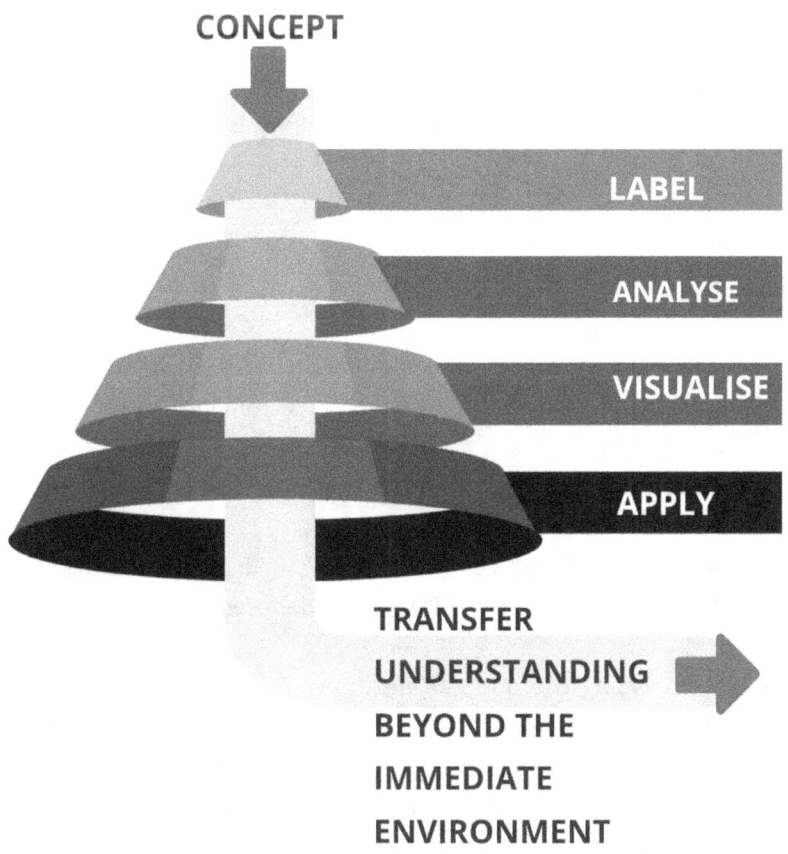

Lava Tube diagram

How are concepts related to family communication? In an earlier chapter, I indicated that I regard communication as a specific type of knowledge. Concepts are the building blocks of communication. Having a deep understanding of the four concepts that follow gives children insights they will use throughout their schooling and lives. Conceptual understanding enriches communication.

I call the concept learning system the LAVA TUBE process. Imagine a lava tube in your mind. It is a geological feature along which the lava flows from deep within a volcano out into the beyond, where over time, it moulds and enriches the landscape. In this way, conceptual understanding flows from knowledge and is applied by children in the real world they inhabit. LAVA TUBE is an acronym for the following:

L – Label
A – Analyse
V – Visualise
A – Apply

TUBE – *T*ransfer the *U*nderstanding *B*eyond the immediate *E*nvironment

Here's a brief description and example of each part to clarify the process.

Label: imagine a child sees a dog. The word 'dog' is a label and the child needs to associate it correctly with what it denotes.

Analyse: analysing the dog can be done in several ways. We can analyse it into whole and parts. The dog is the whole. The body, head, legs, tail, snout, ears, eyes are the parts. We can discuss features of a dog such as size, texture, shape, loudness of the bark. We can talk about a dog's role as a pet and its relationship to human beings. When we analyse, we look at *internal* relationships such as the body connections, and *external* relationships like what a dog means to families and societies.

Visualise: at a first stage, we label and analyse a dog the child can see. The next step is to visualise the dog as representing other dogs, so the child connects this dog to a more universal idea of what dogs are.

Visualising is holding the concept in mind; the ability to concentrate on the mental image of it. This is the art of abstract thinking.

Apply: once the child knows the concept and can visualise it, we might ask them to apply their information and recognise a dog amongst other animals on a page or point them out on a walk to the shops. They can tell you which dogs are cut out to perform skill-related tasks, like sniffer or guide dogs.

Transfer Understanding Beyond the immediate Environment: aligned with visualisation, we want the child to recognise dogs in many different contexts and environments and not only recognise one instance of a dog. This is transfer. Your child might transfer their knowledge to write a story about a mischievous dog or paint a dog from his or her imagination. One of the key goals of education is the transfer of knowledge.

Colour, shape, size and location

Now that you're familiar with the LAVA TUBE process, I'll return to colour, shape, size and location.

The order of presenting these concepts is important and children benefit from a systematic introduction to them in their foundation years of schooling. If your child is entering formal school aged six, then you might like to work through the sequence the year before they enter school.

Let's dive in!

1. Concept-based understanding of colour

I am sure that you are asking yourself why 'colour', such a simple concept, should be highlighted for school age children. Surely even three-year-olds know their colours!?

You are absolutely right. Children can usually identify the colours, especially the primary colours from a very early age. As you will see, concept-based understanding is about more than simply recognising or identifying a colour, or indeed, a shape, size or location. It is having a LAVA TUBE knowledge of the concept.

Over time, you want your children to recognise and label the following categories of colours and individual colours.

- Primary colours
    - Red
    - Yellow
    - Blue

- Secondary colours
    - Green
    - Orange
    - Purple/violet

- Non-spectral colours
    - Brown
    - Black
    - White

- Light and dark shades of colour

How knowledge of colour promotes organised thinking

As important as it is for your child to know these colours, it is *more important* that they know they belong to the category *'colour'*. I've touched on *umbrella concepts* a few times already. Instances of colour such as 'yellow', 'red' and 'blue' belong in a category or class called 'colour'. We cannot recognise something that is 'colour' colour. It is an abstract label for a collection or group of specific colours. The category word 'colour' is like the handle of a suitcase filled with all the words that belong to it. This kind of connective knowledge helps a child to *organise* their thinking hierarchically.

Because colour is so easily accessible and recognisable to young children, it is a great way to commence developing organisation in thinking. If they never connected 'yellow' and 'red' together and never saw the relationship between them, they would have an 'episodic grasp' of reality. They would know every fact they encounter as one isolated idea. But human beings have the great advantage that they can connect ideas through categorisation. There is the overall category colour, and the subcategories: primary, secondary and non-spectral. (You don't have to use the advanced word *non-spectral*, but colours do occur in a spectrum and I feel that if they can name a triceratops or stegosaurus, they can learn advanced terminology!)

Visualisation develops abstract thought

Colour is also an easy entry into abstract thinking. Children learn the difference between concrete 'blue' in the real world and abstract 'blue' in our brains. Human thinking mechanisms and memory are enhanced because of the way we visualise knowledge. Blue occurs as a colour perceptible through our eyes. But the word 'blue' is an arbitrary word/sound to *represent* the blue colour in the spectrum of colours. The colour 'blue' in the world is different from the label 'blue'. To experience blue in reality, we have to see it outside our body. The label 'blue' enables us to visualise it internally. We can talk to one another about it and keep it in memory to think about it. The label *represents* the reality. The minute we *represent* something, we are dealing with abstract thought.

So, when you concentrate on colour as a concept, you will want your child to:

- Recognise and label colours
- Know colours belong to the main category 'colour' and sub-categories primary, secondary and non-spectral
- Be able to visualise and think abstractly about the colour in their minds.

Applying the five-step LAVA TUBE process to colour:
- Label
- Analyse
- Visualise
- Apply knowledge about the concept
- Transfer understanding beyond the immediate environment

L – Label
When you introduce new concepts, don't rush. Don't try and teach all the primary, secondary, non-spectral and shades of colour in one day! Confusion will reign. Introduce the sub-categories in sequence. A good rule of thumb is that if children don't make mistakes when identifying one group, you can move on to the next group.

A – Analyse
To analyse colour, have conversations about it and ask a lot of fun questions. What do you like about the colour yellow? What does the colour blue remind you of? What sound would the colour red make? Which colour is green's best friend? What is the best colour for your cake icing?

When children answer these questions, you are asking them to make *associations*. They connect what they see with what they know and you tantalise their imaginations. There are no right and wrong answers in *associative thinking*. I'm sure you've often seen how associations are instrumental in the flow of conversations. You tell a story and someone else says: 'Oh, that reminds me of … ' and so the conversation goes from one person's associations to another.

V – Visualise
It is vitally important that children learn to visualise information in their minds so they can use it and think about it when it is not immediately present. When they learn about colour, ask your kids to think about objects at school, outside, in their bedroom or somewhere in the

neighbourhood with the colour you're focusing on. This is quite easy with colour, but you can imagine as concepts under consideration get more complex this will be more difficult. Think of fractions. Will they later be able to visualise halves, percentages and ratios? If they get used to *visualising abstractly*, this will be much easier for them later.

A – Apply knowledge about the concept
Once the child knows the focus colour or colours, you can encourage them to identify them in the immediate context. The sofa cushions are blue, the flowers are pink, etc. You can play games and do activities where you sort objects by colour or do puzzles in which colour matching is important. Drawing and painting help consolidate colours and children can have immense fun mixing colours. To see the creation of secondary colours in action, set up a truly wonderful science experiment called 'walking water'.

Walking water

Arrange six small plastic containers filled with water in a circle. Add red food colouring to the first one. Skip a container and add blue food colouring to the third one and finally add yellow food colouring to the fifth one. Fold thick paper towel into strips, just long enough to dip from the middle of one container to the next. Lay six strips across the jars so that the clear water is linked to a coloured water container on either side. Then see what happens! The cellulose in the paper acts like tiny tubules starting off a capillary effect. Primary colours from the jars will 'walk' through the strips to the clear water and create the secondary colours! It's like magic!

TUBE – Transfer understanding beyond the immediate environment.
Transferring information is like taking it across a bridge from one area to another. Over a river, across a ravine. This metaphor is a good way to think about knowledge too. You pack the knowledge into a trunk and travel somewhere else with it. When you have fully explored colour, ask your children where else it is important. Where else can they use the information? I'm sure they'll come up with lots of examples. When you are out and about encourage recognition and meaning of colour wherever you go. Flags, footy colours, traffic lights, road signs or the sky in different weather conditions.

Modes of thinking uncovered when considering the concept of colour

Three focal types of thinking we have uncovered talking about colour are *organised thinking*, how things belong and are ordered, *associative thinking*, how one idea triggers another and *abstract thinking*, holding and using ideas in the mind. But as you discuss colour you encourage several other thinking techniques: focus, labelling, attention, comparison and using logical evidence. These are all excellent tools of the mind.

2. Concept-based understanding of shape
Shape is a fundamental mathematical concept

Teaching shape IS the job of your children's teachers, but you have the advantage that you can provide the correct language whenever you encounter shapes in real life. This is often much more effective than when children are introduced to them in a theoretical way in the classroom. Over time, you want your children to recognise the following groups of shapes.

- Linear shapes
  - Straight line shape
  - Curved line shape (arc, bowed/curved, arch)
  - Angle shape

- Two-dimensional shapes
  - Round (circle, oval)
  - Square (rectangle family)
  - Triangular (triangle)
  - Diamond (rhombus)

- Three-dimensional shape
  - Cubic (cube)
  - Spherical (ball, sphere)
  - Conical (cone)
  - Cylindrical (cylinder)

- Other common shapes
  - Egg shape
  - Star shape
  - Moon (crescent) shape

As for colour, in shape we also use the LAVA TUBE process:

- Label
- Analyse
- Visualise
- Apply knowledge about the concept
- Transfer understanding beyond the immediate environment.

Once you and your child know the LAVA TUBE sequence well, the steps can be combined. Often you will be providing labels and analysing, visualising or transferring at the same time. But don't do this before they are clear on what each step entails.

L – Label

The common geometric shapes kids learn at school are called universal shapes. As with colour, don't introduce shapes all at once! Introduce the two-dimensional ones slowly and then move onto the three-dimensional. They need to know more about the shapes than simply recognising them. You can introduce them to the features of each shape at the level of their capability.

A – Analyse

To do any good analysis of something, you need to identify its features. Different shapes have different features. I would start with round shapes. Don't only offer your child a circle to represent round shape. Oval shapes and parts of shapes, like semi-circles, also have the characteristic of roundness. Plates, saucers, wheels, parts of toys, even movements like spinning can demonstrate roundness. If you offer only one example and only in one context, children don't transfer their knowledge easily.

After round shapes, move onto the line shapes.

When you teach young children about a square it is enough for them to:

- identify it by appearance
- say that it has four corners
- say that the four sides are straight
- can count the sides and corners.

What you are attuning them to in these ideas are the *features* of the shape. Circles don't have corners, but squares do. It is *comparison of the features* of different things that will enable them to systematically distinguish between them. How is a square different from a pentagon? If the children know the *features*, they see that both are linear, have straight sides and corners. But they notice that the square has four sides and the pentagon, five, that the corners in the pentagon are not right angles.

The more precisely children can articulate the differences in maths and indeed in all their subject areas, and the more detailed their knowledge, the more successful they will be at scholastic tasks. Multiple exam and test questions will ask children to compare things. Because they will be used to *identifying the features* and *comparing them systematically*, they will provide highly skilled answers.

Don't move from the square to the pentagon until the children have fully internalised the square.

Have some fun with the square by hunting for right angles.

> Children can know what a right angle is without knowing that it is 90°. Pin two strips of paper together with a split pin so kids can adjust the angle, they can have fun opening it up to match all the corners in the room. Soon they will have a visual idea of what 90° looks like. It's easier to learn about right angles when you know what a corner looks and feels like.

A colleague of mine tells a lovely story about her grandson when she was exploring right angles. She held up her hand with thumb and index finger in an L-shape and told him, you always have a right angle you can use to compare things to. A day or two later, he dutifully held up his right hand in the L shape declaring, 'here is my right angle', then without hesitation held up his other hand with an L-shape and said proudly, 'and here is my left angle'. You never know how kids are processing things, do you?

Once children have internalised the easy features, move onto more difficult language. Introduce labels like vertical, horizontal and diagonal. That sets them up to discuss with authority features of other more complex line shapes like the pentagon already discussed, octagons, triangles and dodecagons!

TUBE – Transfer understanding beyond the immediate environment

Once children know that features are important for identifying and understanding things, they are in a much greater position to visualise, generalise, use and transfer that knowledge.

You can ask them why tyres are round, buildings vertical and why squares fit together with triangles more easily than with circles?

As with colour, make your children aware of shape when you are out and about.

Many patterns are made up of shapes. Get kids to describe patterns on walls, fences, windows, logos or adverts. Encourage them to use adjectives like vertical, horizontal, diagonal and perpendicular, sequenced, recurring, arranged and other vocabulary for describing geometric patterns with precision.

Analytical thinking

The specific kind of thinking surfaced when we discuss shape is *analytical thinking* which requires awareness of *features* of things and the *internal and external relationships* related to them.

Two individual thinking skills they use in analysis are comparison and logical reasoning.

3. Concept-based understanding of size

Size, like shape and position, is an important mathematical idea. Big, small and medium are great words, but I encourage you to use a much broader vocabulary. Identify things as gigantic, miniscule, tiny, immense, massive or microscopic.

Size introduces relative thinking

Introduce the idea that size is relative. Collect three different-sized stones. Select two and ask which is bigger. Encourage a justification. Then produce the third stone. You kids might have to alter their decision because the third stone might be the biggest, the middle-sized, or the smallest. Working with more than two sizes introduces superlatives. Big, bigger, biggest. Superlatives are regularly embedded in word problems, for example, 'What was the age of the tallest boy?'

L – Label

Below are some relative or comparative size concepts to explore:

- big
- medium
- small
- bigger
- smaller
- long
- short
- longer
- shorter
- taller
- heavier
- lighter
- more
- less.

These words are comparative, or relative concepts, not precise. Precision is introduced when we measure size in units. When children are able, you can advance, and introduce them to the units that measure different dimensions.

Measuring in precise units

We measure lines, or linear dimensions in metres and parts of metres: millimetres, centimetres, metres, kilometres. Units of measurement change depending on what we are measuring:

- length
- width

- height
- depth
- circumference
- diameter
- perimeter
- distance.

Introduce kids to how this differs across substances and materials:

- liquids are measured in litres (volume)
- weight is measured in grams (weight).

A – Analyse

Size is only one thing that can be measured and for which specific units of measurement have been derived. Eventually your kids will measure time, direction, speed, decibels, angles, velocity, rates of change and statistical data! We call this broad measuring *quantification*.

Understanding *equal, more and less* and working with *units of measurement*, your child is more likely to stay the course in STEM subjects (science, technology, engineering and maths). This is because they'll know that we measure specific dimensions in specific units. Sometimes as learning becomes more complex, they must combine the units. In speed, both time and distance are required, so we get metres per second. Imagine how ahead of the game they will be if they are *slowly* introduced to all these ideas in the real world as they spend time with you. I was delighted the other day when I heard a child yell out to her dad, 'Stop, the tyres have reached 32 psi!' I had to look up the name of the unit to find it meant pounds per square inch. Old imperial measurements are still in use!

As you walk, drive, tram or trek, discuss how things are measured. Distance, time, weight, temperature, pressure, speed, direction, angles and for the petrol heads in your family, horsepower and acceleration.

And as mentioned above, psi or kPa make much more sense to kids who monitor the air pump at the service station. Kilometres, millimetres, kilograms, milligrams, degrees, hours, minutes and seconds are much more relevant, when you talk about them in real life.

V – Visualise

Giving children real world experience with sizes, helps them to consider size in abstract problems like the tricky word problems they will encounter in the classroom. John is 20cm taller than his brother. Sarah, the tallest of three sisters, is 10cm shorter than John. Who is taller, John's brother or Sarah? What is the height difference between them?

A – Apply

The older children in the five to nine age group might like to have fun measuring perimeters and exploring area. As stressed before active involvement supports conceptual understanding.

The perimeter is the distance around the object. For example, if your house has a fenced yard, the perimeter is the length of the fence. This is a one-dimensional line. When you go walking declare, 'let's do the perimeter of the park!' Kids need to learn how one-dimensional linear measurements, length, are different from two dimensional measurements, area.

When your child is asked at school to measure the perimeter of a square, they are taught to add the length of the four sides together or multiply the length of one side by four. Perimeter is measured in centimetres or metres.

When we measure surface area, we use metres squared (m2), length x width. And when we measure three-dimensional objects, we use metres cubed (m3), length x width x height.

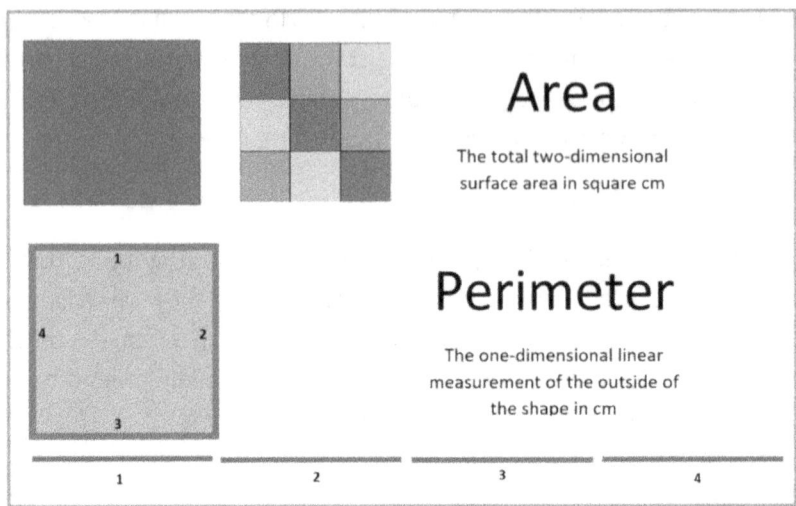

Perimeter versus area

Give your kids practice using string to measure the perimeter of objects in the house like a table-top, the TV, a trampoline, etc. At the same time teach them about circumference and measure the outside of a round pot, or old-fashioned CD.

Area
They can use square paper cut-outs to build up the area of shapes. They can say the area of the square took 9, or 12, or 16 smaller squares. This practice is excellent because they are using their hands, eyes and brains to internalise the concepts.

Understanding perimeter and area will make it much easier when they hit three-dimensional mathematics.

Seriation
Seriation is arranging things in increasing or decreasing order. Children enjoy practising this idea with all kinds of toys and materials at home. They can order themselves by height with their friends, weigh materials

and create a graph representing the objects from lightest to heaviest. Ordering by size with concrete objects is preparation for doing this kind or ordering with more abstract concepts like speed. You might help them create a graph capturing the results of an experiment with balls rolling down a plank. As you change the angle of the plank by 3cm as it rests against the sofa, how much further does the ball travel?

Seriation

What's more, they will be able to relate seriation to abstract concepts like importance. Which part of this story is the most important? Can you arrange these five ideas from the most important to the least important? Which is the most important piece of information you need to know before you can solve this problem?

TUBE – Transfer beyond the immediate environment
Children will find an infinite number of ways to apply their knowledge about size, measurement and units. And the knowledge will set them up to approach multiple kinds of tasks and problems. In the kitchen or garage, invite your children to measure and vocalise the units like weight, length, angle, volume or speed. They will certainly thank you for their precision of expression.

Relative thinking

The kind of thinking highlighted in size is *relative thinking*. Dimension always measures one thing in relation to something else.

You will find you use relative thinking in many ways yourself outside of mathematics too. You might assess how important a particular experience in your past was in shaping who you are today. To do that you have to assess it relative to all the other collective experiences.

4. Concept-based understanding of location

Location is also a fundamental mathematical concept. This concept will be introduced with the same LAVA TUBE process.

Position is a fixed location

To be clear, position is generally a fixed point. When something is moving, the concept we have to use is 'direction'. We use the compass points for position and also for direction. Position and direction both come under the description 'orientation in space'. When talking about compass points in position, something might be located to the north of something else. The vocabulary your child should become familiar with over time is listed below.

L – Label

Expose your children to the following position ideas:

- body positions: sitting, lying, standing, kneeling
- place positions: on, over, above, in front, behind, under, beside/next to, between, inside, outside, on the right, on the left
- linear positions: horizontal position, vertical/perpendicular position, diagonal/at an angle/slanting position
- direction: to the north, to the south, to the west, to the east.

You will notice that these concept labels range from simple to more advanced. But there are similarities across the types. For instance, a 'standing' position is also 'vertical'; and 'lying' is generally 'horizontal'.

When your young children are introduced to the body positions, they are internalising ideas that will continue to develop and be refined later.

Reference points in space

No position can be discussed without reference to something else. There are two main kinds of reference points: perspectival and universal (or fixed) reference points.

A – Analyse

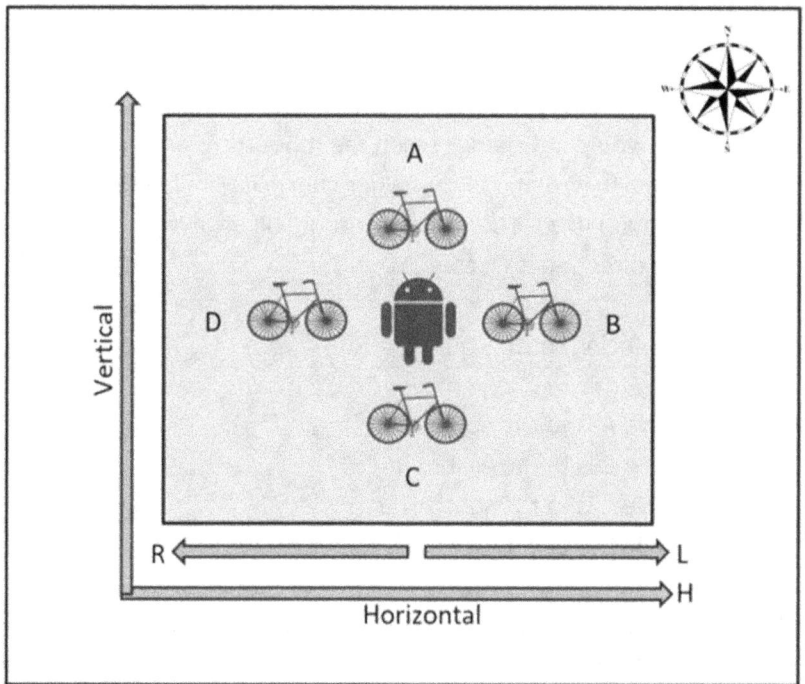

Perspectival reference points

In this diagram, the robot figure is facing us, and we are facing it. The position of the four bicycles will be described in relation to its perspective. There is a convention in drawings that what appears above an object, as in this representation, is behind it; and what is below is in front.

When we analyse this diagram from the robot's perspective:

- Bicycle A is behind it
- Bicycle B is to the left of it
- Bicycle C is in front of it
- Bicycle D is to the right of it.

When we look at the picture, Bicycle B is to our right, the opposite of the robot – but if the robot turned around, all these positions would change.

Universal reference points

If we assume that the robot is facing south, then we can talk about where the bicycles are in relation to the fixed or universal compass points. These would not change when the robot turns around. Once we know where north is, that is always where north is. Similarly vertical and horizontal remain fixed. The standing robot will always be vertical, no matter which direction it faces.

If the robot is facing south:

- Bicycle A is to the north of it
- Bicycle B is to the east of it
- Bicycle C is to the south of it
- Bicycle D is to the west of it.

When we look at the picture, our reference to the fixed compass points is identical to the robot's – and if the robot turned around, all the compass point position would remain the same.

Position is related to direction

As indicated above position and direction both come under the superordinate concept: orientation. It is worthwhile to have a look at the concept system for direction here.

General direction concepts:

- moving forwards or backwards
- moving towards the right or left
- moving up/upwards or down/downwards
- moving towards or away from something
- moving alongside beside something
- moving sideways to the left or the right.

Compass directions:

- moving to the south/southward/southbound; or north/northward/northbound
- moving to the east/eastward/eastbound; west/westward/westbound
- there are other compass points like north-east, etc. to learn at a later stage.

When we talk about wind:

- moving away from the north/northerly
- moving away from the south/southerly
- moving away from the west/westerly
- moving away from the east/easterly.

V-Visualise

It is very important for children to visualise where things are in space. Ask them to imagine their hats in the top shelf of their cupboards and their shoes on the bottom. Ask them to imagine and describe the route to get from home to school and then again in reverse. The ability to transform things spatially in the mind is crucially important for abstract thinking. Many aspects of mathematics including graphing, representing arithmetic processes and fractions rely on an understanding of space and direction.

A – Apply

When you go on a walk, allow your children to map your route and encourage the use of all the language of space. Up, down, in, out, under, over, above, below, between, around, within, beside. Every time you go out, make sure children verbalise these terms. Each of us has a dominant side. As early as possible assist your child to identify their dominant side and name it so they can use it as a reference for left and right. Get them to verbalise the instructions for the family and describe what is around them in precise language. They might say, 'the tree is on my right now, but soon it will be on the right and behind me'. Or, 'I can see a huge gum tree on the eastern perimeter of the park.' Give fun instructions as you walk. Take three steps forward, turn to your left and hop three times. Jump backwards on both legs and bend down to touch the ground. The more kids feel these reference points in their bodies, the better they will understand them. When they are ready, take a compass along and teach them about north, south, east and west.

Thinking modes related to position

The specific kind of thinking when we talk about position and direction is *perspectival thinking*. Your child learns to take note of the point of view. They learn to be flexible in understanding that left and right change depending on relative positions. But the compass points are fixed and don't change around.

TUBE – Transfer understanding beyond the immediate environment

Perspective taking is one of the most important thinking skills you can assist your child to develop. In more abstract ways later on, if they are aware of these perspectival shifts, they will be able to assess characters' experiences in their reading materials, understand different perspective across history and understand where people are coming from as they voice their opinions. They will be much more open-minded and receptive to different arguments and be much better and more critical thinkers throughout their lives.

There are innumerable concepts besides those introduced here, but I am sure that as we have dealt with each of these concepts, you have seen how functional they are in enabling children to unpack and repack, decode and encode information in all their school subjects as well as in their daily lives and sporting pursuits.

Here's a brief summary of types of thinking related to each of the concepts:

Colour	Organised, Abstract, Associative
Shape	Organised, Abstract, Analytical
Size	Organised, Abstract, Relative
Position	Organised, Abstract, Perspectival

Reading and writing

Now that you've got the four concepts: colour, shape, size and position under your belt, we can consider ways to introduce children formally to reading and writing.

Letters and the conservation of constancy
Letters are the building blocks of spoken and written language – yet there is no one way to represent the 26 letters of the English alphabet.

The first point of confusion for children is that we have capital and lower-case letters. Besides the different cases, letters appear in the environment in different fonts, styles and designs. They also occur in cursive and print! This can be extremely overwhelming for children because it's impossible to predict when and where they will be called on to decode all these different versions.

If children learn right from the outset, that letters have an identity, but that they can change both their appearance and their sound we will make it easier for them to cope with all the variations.

The reason for presenting colour, shape, size and position earlier is that these concepts can now be harnessed to make your child's letter and sound learning much more systematic. They can use their experience of comparison and all the terminology we discussed to help them with their alphabet.

When you introduce letters, talk about human qualities. Here is the letter 'A'. This is also letter 'A', but it looks like this 'a'. They look different because sometimes they have different jobs. Think of yourself. When you go to school you wear your uniform and when you go out, you wear your jeans and T-shirt. You look different, but it's still you!

Intrinsic to what I have just described is that children need to learn *conservation of constancy in letters*. In the example of school uniform and going out clothes, what remains constant is the identity of the child. So it is with letters. Even when shape, size, orientation or position changes, the identity of the letter is constant.

Stick to the visual appearance of letters before introducing their sounds

I would stick with appearance, the visual aspect of letters, before focusing on sounds. Of course, sound is already happening when you name the letters. Really ensure they know what the letters look like and even be able to copy or draw them before you concentrate too much on the complexity of sounds.

But when you do introduce sounds, the same thing applies. When you attribute a sound to the letter, you can say that on most occasions when we see the letter it has a particular sound, but that sometimes it will change its voice. Sometimes, when it works together with other letters, it will sound different, but it is always 'A'.

As you introduce this idea of the conservation of constancy, or the constant identity of the letter in different representations, sounds and partnerships you can make it fun for kids. Your child might create a special dossier for each letter where they collect its variations but maintain its integrity and identity. In the below infographic, some ideas related to the conservation of constancy of letters are shown.

 # Letter 'A' Fun Facts

The letter 'A' has a capital and small letter: 'A' and 'a'. These forms have different jobs and the capital 'A' likes to be at the beginning of sentences and the beginning of names! All 26 letters have capital and lower case letters!

The more letters we know, the more words we can make! Start with very short words like bat, mat, cat, hat, fat, sat. Then go on to the longer words like 'apple'. Did you notice some letters like to double up? like 'P' in 'apple'?

I wonder how you might like to build the letter 'A'? You can do its capital and lower case. What would 'A' look like in clay? Hey, that rhymes! What other words, rhyme with clay?! Most letters are made with either straight or round shapes.

The letter 'A' likes to team up with other letters to make new sounds. 'E' is a favourite. Together 'E' and 'A' make the sound 'EE', like in team! When 'A' is next to 'R' it often changes its sound to 'AAH', like in far. Just like you, letters have some favourite friends!

The more letters we know, the more words we can make! Start with very short words like bat, mat, cat, hat, fat, sat. Then go on to the longer words like 'apple'. Did you notice some letters like to double up? like 'P' in 'apple'?

When we learn our 26 letters, we have to be great detectives to see how they work on their own and work together. And we have to know ALL the different sounds each letter can make!

Most of these facts apply to the other letters too!

Reading infographic

Shape, size, position and orientation of letters

Letters all have features of shape, size, position and orientation. For each letter, children must know these in order to accomplish the precision and accuracy required for good writing.

It is strategic to commence teaching the capital letters that all have straight lines. Most capitals can be built with four long lines and three short lines. Try this with matchsticks or paper drinking straws. Have two whole ones and then snip two in half.

How many of these can you build?

A B C D E F G H I J K L M N O P Q R S T U V W X Y Z

The letters you can't build with sticks, have curves or round shapes.

What about the lower case?

a b c d e f g h i j k l m n o p q r s t u v w x y z

The lower case has many more rounded shapes and the position and orientation are more complex than the capitals.

We often use strategies like holding up the hands to help children with reversal issues. This is the shape for 'bed':

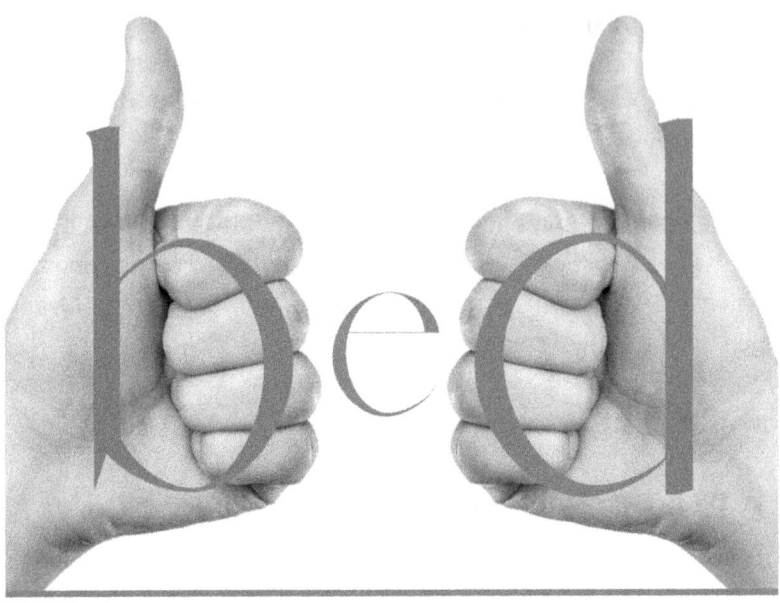

Trick to correct 'b and d' reversal

This is not incorrect and will be helpful to children, but we want to embed directionality at a deeper level and within their own bodies. And of course, if you've followed the advice in the book, you will already have worked on left and right.

Left-right dominance
Rather than teaching children tricks and tips it's worth spending time working with children to recognise their own left or right dominance so that they can genuinely know which is their left and right from an internal place within their own body. This is deeper more enduring learning than looking to clues in the environment to assist them.

Oral versus written language
One of the key things to do to support your children's literacy has already been flagged and that is reading with and to them. I love the quote by Annie Proulx below, because it goes to the heart of the matter.

> 'You should write because you love the shape of stories and sentences and the creation of different words on a page. Writing comes from reading, and reading is the finest teacher of how to write.'
> ## Annie Proulx

And equally important to reading is talking to them.

Reading and writing are very technical and can be taught in a technical way. But much more important than recognising, sounding or forming letters is *having something to say*! If you have rich conversations with your children, they will have rich thoughts and rich ideas.

Quite often on a Monday in the Preparatory classroom the teacher will say, take out your journal and write about what you did at the weekend. The new writer will start off in poor spelling: *At the wknd we wnt fisin wit dad.*

It will take a half hour. The book is collected and marked. Teachers these days have the grace to desist from scrawling red corrections over the work, but I'm really not sure what this activity achieves?

If you ask the same child to *tell* you about the weekend, you might get:

> 'We hopped in the car on Friday and drove to Phillip Island. We stayed over at Grandma's and had pie and chips for dinner. We watched Spiderman 3, put on our jim-jams and jumped into bed. On Saturday Dad took us out in the boat fishing. He put the bait on the hook for us. We caught a King George whiting and Dad hooked into a flathead but lost it. We also found a heap of abalone shells. That was really sad because abalone are protected and someone broke the law. You're not allowed to take them out.'

There is an incredible difference between what children know in their early school years, and what they can write.

I believe in practising writing. But perhaps, once you've listened and possibly even scribed for them, select three words, or one sentence and work on it together.

To summarise ideas about learning letters, here are 12 key things you can teach them over time about reading and writing. (Of course, you won't sit them down and teach them the whole list in the first hour!)

1. There are only 26 letters and you can learn them easily
2. They occur in pairs: each letter has a capital and a lower case
3. They have different shapes, but in general they are made of rounded shapes and line shapes
4. When we use letters, they represent sounds
5. We use letters to make words
6. Sometimes the letters team up to make a different sound, or change each other's sounds
7. Sometimes the same letters make different sounds in different words
8. Fifteen of the capital letters can be made from three straws and three half straws
9. Eleven of the capital letters are formed from a combination of lines and rounded shapes
10. Sometimes the letters are written or typed in different ways, but they're still the same letter
11. There are five vowels and 21 consonants
12. Occasionally a consonant sounds like a vowel.

You can have fun with the letters at home without expecting children to learn to read immediately.

There are so many commercial letters available. You can get wooden or plastic ones. But my experience is that there are never enough of a particular letter in these boxes for children to create all the words or play the games they want to. So, a suggestion is to just create a word table of capital and lowercase letters on the computer and print them off. You can put 13 letters on each of four pages. You can start each alphabet playtime by getting them to help you sort them out. Then put all the vowels on one side.

Playfully introduce the children to the names of the letters. Do this in groups of two to three letters at a time. Not too overwhelming. Move onto new letters when children have consolidated the ones you introduced at first. When you add more, go back and ensure they are all being maintained in long-term memory. Counter to a lot of current practices, I suggest teaching the capital letters first. Children seem to be drawn to them. Then teach them to match each capital with its lower-case partner by sight. If sound comes into it, that is fine, but the emphasis should be on the visual recognition and naming of capital and its lower-case equivalent. Use the names, not the sounds, A B C, (not ah bah kah).

When you focus on sounds later, do it with both the capital and lowercase together.

This capital letter 'A' and the little letter 'a' usually say 'a', like in apple. But in some words, like in far, they can say 'aah' and in another word like hay, they say 'ay'. Can you say a, aah, ay?

Let's build two words where the A says 'a'. Here we go: bat, mat.

Go through the sounds focusing on the vowels. As you do that you can refer to the sounds of the consonants but make the vowels the main focus.

Am I asking you to take over teaching literacy from the teacher? Yes and no. The teacher will have his or her own way of teaching reading and writing, but this playful experience and the general knowledge about the alphabet and how it works can avoid a lot of confusion. Besides I think your child might enjoy this connective general information about how letters work.

If a child can learn the names of a gazillion Pokémon characters and a bunch of extinct dinosaurs, they can surely master 26 letters of the alphabet. Especially after the grounding they have in shape, size and position you will have worked on before letters.

Before we look at numbers, here's a summary of the key points on reading and writing:

- language structures are hierarchical and a letter is the initial building block
- letter formation is a highly complex task that harnesses knowledge of shape, size and position
- letters represent sounds and combine to make meanings
- students need to understand the conservation of constancy between the capital and lower-case letters
- conservation of constancy also applies as different fonts, printing and cursive writing are encountered
- together letters combine to form the basis of all verbal language
- letters share common features with the writing of numbers
- reading and writing are at the very tip of an extensive literacy iceberg
- children need to internalise many spatial concepts including their left or right dominance to write successfully
- children's writing ability is not as competent in the initial stages as their oral language
- give children opportunities to explain things orally and scribe their words for them. Practise a section of what they have contributed as a writing experience.

Number concepts

Eighty percent of the population is traumatised by mathematics at school. Whether you were or not, you want to develop a positive attitude to maths in your kids by exploring it in fun, relaxed ways. Here are some ideas.

Talk positively about maths! Never say maths is difficult or you hate it. If you do, your children could adopt your beliefs and be disadvantaged before they begin.

Upscale maths vocabulary. Most maths difficulties occur because children don't understand the question. If they don't understand terminology, they lose their way. So, when you have the opportunity to use mathematical language, include it in a sentence. You might say, 'Let's go for a walk around the *perimeter* of the park', or 'You can have half the pizza. That's 50%!'

Provide fun hands-on maths activities. The number system is complex, but the foundation of numbers is that they tell us if things are equal, or more or less.

Sort, match and group

Putting things in groups without getting too fussed about counting is a good way to start maths thinking. The early years are the perfect time to match, sort, group, estimate and begin counting. The more hands-on experience your child gets the better they'll understand how to quantify anything in the world around them. Don't overwhelm them or try to teach number too fast. As mentioned before, you don't want to imprint negative experience with learning. You will want your child to LOVE maths. Get out your button box, sort the cutlery, sort the groceries, sort their clothes as they pack them away. When they do this, they practise decision-making based on what they observe about what is the same and what is different. As they advance and number is introduced, they graduate these ideas to their understanding of number. How are they the same and different; how are they more or less?

To match they must understand why things belong in categories. Out shopping, make a game of finding things. 'Lead me to the milk, a 10m roll of aluminium foil or one of those six-packs of pink lady apples for your lunch boxes.' They'll apply memory and logic to locate the items. Have younger children scan the shelf for something familiar by colour and shape – and allow them to see it first!

Counting

The concepts, more, less and equivalent are foundational to understanding the number system. With very young children, before introducing the first numbers, these foundational concepts need to be in place. Once they start to count, count everything! Stairs, paces, paving stones. Once kids count confidently, collect groups of 10. 'How many groups of 10 trees or lamp posts will we pass between here and our place?' This consolidates base 10 maths, memory and recall.

Children need three important number skills. Count the numbers in the correct order, have one-to-one correspondence, and 'count on'. Each tree they pass can be allocated a different number. You can exercise 'counting on' by saying, 'We have passed five trees, what number is the next one?'.

The value-add to your child's negotiation of maths using these fun foundations, will be incalculable.

Proportion

Equivalence, proportion and ratio are advanced terms, but the concepts can be introduced early on in a variety of ways with very young children. Proportion is a foundational and is based on the concepts of equal, more and less. Simple activities like pouring different levels of coloured water into two identical containers and asking your child to tell which has more or less, is a good way to start working with these ideas.

Proportion measures a part compared to the whole. Proportions can be expressed in fractions. At breakfast ask children to quantify how much orange juice they have in their glass. More or less than half? How much more than half? Get the measuring jug out and find out what is exactly half. Proportion is the basis of fractions, ratios, percentages and decimals. When the pizza arrives, talk about how many pieces make a half. Concentrate on one fraction at a time. Consolidate halves in several different contexts before introducing quarters or eighths, for example, 'we are halfway there', 'get me a half a cup of sugar for this recipe', 'you've done half your homework'. Chatting about halves (and later other fractions) proves that maths is a widely applicable, real-world thing.

More advanced grouping
Once children have mastered grouping according to shape or colour, and they are counting well, you can challenge them to group by number. Start off putting simple objects in groups with low numbers of 1–5. When the children master these numbers, do 1–10 and so on.

Get children to create:

- groups that are equal or not equal in number
- groups of singles, tens, hundreds, etc. (depending on the education level of the student)
- larger or smaller groups in comparison with a reference group
- fractions or parts of whole numbers (depending on the education level of the student).

Get children to analyse pictures using their number knowledge.

Set out some blocks of different shapes, colours and sizes. Then analyse the array. How many blue blocks are there? Which colour has the most blocks? Are there more triangles or cylinders? Which shape groups have more than three in the group? In the last question, the children need to talk about number in relation to two concepts, groups and contents of the groups.

Three types of number concepts

It will benefit kids to know the different ways numbers are used.

Cardinal: number. This relates to how many there are. Each number has a value 1, 2, 3 ... etc. In the example above we count the number of blocks. If a cardinal number has a value of one, it is a precise value and it is able to determine whether something is more, less or equal related to that value.

Ordinal: position. The ordinal number indicates the position order of an object or other entity and we use the terms first, second, third, etc.

Nominal: name. Nominal is when a number is used to designate and name something, for example a player in a team. Number 1 is Harry Jones. You can ask someone to go and get the bucket labelled 1. A house number similarly is designated a number name to enable people to find it in the street.

Sequencing – ordering time
Sequencing is similar to seriation which you encountered when we discussed size, but it relates not to dimensional order, but to time order. Which thing came first, second, etc. Also, the idea of beginning, middle and end. When students have this knowledge, they can make sense of what is happening when they read a story. This is called 'monitoring' when we talk about comprehension in literacy contexts. They use sequencing when they plan their activities and when determining the order of steps in a problem. Number concepts are the basis of sequencing.

As with literacy, there are multiple ways children can practise number and mathematics.

Symbolic thinking
Earlier, I introduced the kinds of thinking related to four concepts. Reading and maths introduce a further level, symbolic thinking. This is where a

symbol, like a number, or letter represents something else. A number represents a value and a letter represents a sound.

Attune children to three kinds of language
In the discussion about conceptual understanding, I am sure you recognise three kinds of language.

Specific language describes what is available and visible in the immediate situation. For example, a specific visible dining table is in view and referred to if you ask a child to 'please set the table'.

Conceptual language is visualising a table that may not be present and which represents all tables. Concepts allow us to think about anything, anywhere. They are abstract and universal.

Cognitive language refers to the thinking process used to talk and think about the world around us. It refers to verbs like, think, decide, imagine, plan, compare, observe and hypothesise. The more children know about how they are thinking the more efficient their thinking will become.

We can use the ruler below to demonstrate the three kinds of language.

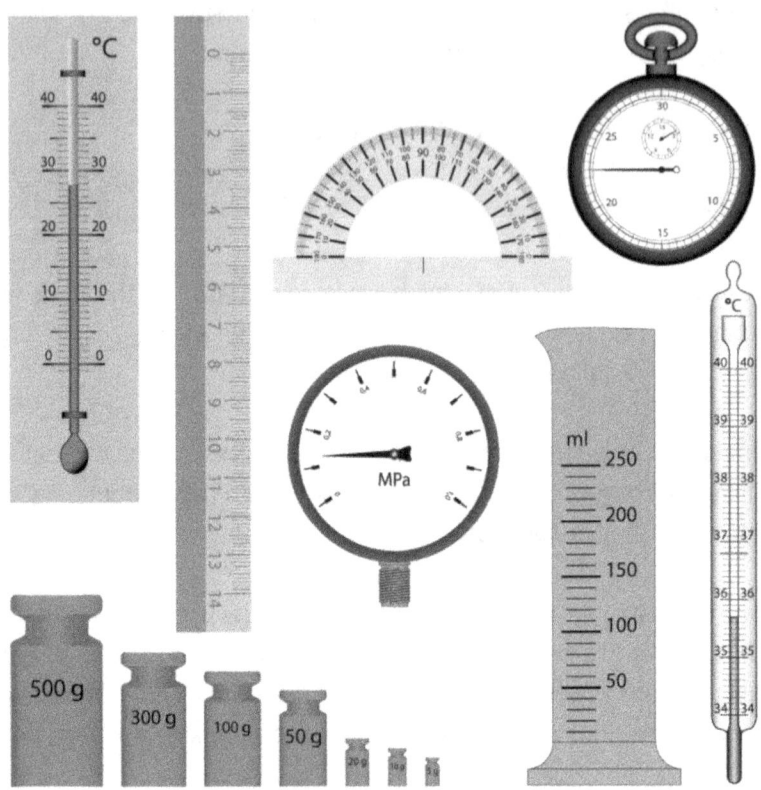

Ruler as example of measuring tools

If a child learns a label as we've discussed, perhaps a 'ruler', that is a single situation-bound experience. This single, specific situation bound language is episodic and unconnected to other language. It is difficult to transfer to new contexts without deeper understanding.

When the child learns that the ruler is a tool for measuring things, he or she sees it as connected to other things. They acquire conceptual understanding. At this level, the ruler is linked to more universal and general knowledge. This enables the child to visualise and entertain thoughts about a ruler, its uses, appearance, connection to other things within their own mind. This knowledge is connected, transferable and available in new contexts.

Metacognition – thinking about thinking

We have also spoken often about the use of processes for thinking, or cognitive language. When a child knows that they can connect, categorise, compare, plan, imagine, hypothesise about things, they are in touch with their own thinking processes.

IN SUMMARY:

- Substantial preliteracy skills are consolidated prior to formal schooling, but in the first years of formal education, the key focus is on reading and writing
- Crucial language learning at school is more than acquiring new vocabulary
- Junior primary is a time for mastering abstract thinking, consolidating concepts and developing conceptual understanding i.e., knowing the relationships between and among whatever children are observing or thinking about
- Knowing an isolated concept is no longer enough, children need to understand how concepts are connected, related, mobilised and used
- A child benefits when parents maintain their role as primary educator and supplement school learning with attention to concepts in everyday life
- The parent or primary caregiver is not a traditional teacher but a mediator of learning. A mediator walks beside a child, not pulling them along nor pushing from behind
- Mediation has three parameters: the learning should be intentional on behalf of the parent, but the child ought to reciprocate. The child should understand the purpose of the learning. The learning is most effective if the concepts learned are bridged to other situations
- The five-step LAVA TUBE method for introducing concepts is an acronym for: Label, Analyse, Visualise, Apply and Transfer Understanding Beyond the immediate Environment
- In this section, four concepts are introduced in a structured way: colour, shape, size and position
- These concepts introduce specific modes of thinking and they help to develop reading and writing

- Early reading and writing are easier if children understand that letters have a name and a sound, that each letter has an upper and lower case and they can look different. It helps if children learn that the letter remains constant, even if it looks and sounds different
- There are three different kinds of number children might become familiar with: cardinal, ordinal and nominal. Cardinal is an absolute value; ordinal indicates a position in a sequence; and nominal is when a number acts as a label
- The concepts discussed and letters and numbers are related to different kinds of thinking: organised, associative, abstract, analytical, relational, perspectival and symbolic
- The junior primary years are important for broadening interests and encouraging creative projects
- There are low and high order concepts. Single instances like rain, snow, mist and fog are low order concepts belonging to a category or high order concept, weather. The high order concepts are called umbrella concepts in the text. Umbrella concepts support organised thinking, memory and the efficient recall or information
- When children develop expertise in their area of interest and acquire creative and design skills, they are building self-mastery a key element of self-actualisation.

Tweens and teens

CHAPTER FIVE

Beyond the Family: Stepping into the Neighbourhood Senior Primary and Secondary (9 to 17 years)

'Who in the world am I? Ah, that's the great puzzle!'
Alice in Wonderland, Lewis Carroll

There was a legendary long weekend in Perth that comes up often in conversation. And no, it was not a pleasant highlight. It was the weekend my daughter, Candice, used up her entire arsenal of teenage horridness. She wanted to spend Easter with friends on a farm near Melbourne. It is likely it had more to do with a handsome young man than her girlfriends but that's beside the point. Pierre and I were planning a trip to Perth for golf. Sean being five years older was doing his own thing. From our perspective, Candice's arrangements didn't concretise quickly enough, so we included her in our plans and booked the flights. We thought we were being perfectly reasonable. Candice did not! She said there was more than enough time for us to wait for her plans to be finalised. She felt, and likely still does, that our decision was pre-emptive, disrespectful and left her without a choice. She tells us to this day it was the most unfair thing we ever did and describes it as 'flipping stubborn for no good reason'. With this antipathy on both sides, we were in for a really lovely time. Not.

We got hot tongue and cold shoulder for four days. From affable and lovely she became vile and poisonous. No matter what we did or said it wasn't good enough. We felt like we were cats with long tails in a room full of rocking chairs, never knowing what she was going to say or do next. It all came to a head on the Sunday when we'd planned to cycle along the Swan River something I'd wanted to do for years. And still have not done. At the point of hiring the bikes we somehow got the straw (or comment) that broke the camel's back. Pierre turned on his heel and went back to the car. Then I lost it! In effect, I said that if this was the way she was going to deal with every disappointment in her life, she was doomed to misery. (Maybe in not such genteel words.)

We motored down to Fremantle gritting our teeth, and on the way she apologised. Then we all apologised. We actually had a great two hours at a street fair before travelling to the airport to fly home. I think we all learned a lot from that weekend. Candice has been affable and lovely ever since (well mostly) and now takes this as a great story, even pivotal.

Apologies and forgiveness might not always come as quickly as this in life, (and maybe it's an assumption we're forgiven), but they are important ways to get over the speedbumps life puts in the way of harmony. With tongue in cheek apologies to Jim Hanson's frog, Kermit, 'It's not easy being tween!'

Focal area of development

The pre-adolescent and adolescent years are a time when young people are forming their personal identities. The experience can be as confusing for them as it is for you. You may find your suggestable, affectionate child morphs into a disagreeable, monosyllabic grunter. Tweens, and even more so teens, want to spend most of their time with their friends. They may not want to be seen with you, let alone talk to you! Because of physical and allied emotional changes, older kids seek privacy and prefer others not to invade their space.

Puberty

There is evidence that children are reaching puberty with all its attendant issues at a younger age than in past decades (Epstein, 2019). As in the preschool years, when children mature in advance of their peers in some respects, tweens might stand out and attract attention if their physical maturity runs ahead of their social and cognitive development. The reasons cited for current earlier maturity in children are many and varied including diet, body mass index, additives in food and cosmetics and genes.

In the industrial 1880s when food was scarce and life unpredictable, the onset of puberty occurred as late as 15 years but in the western world where food is available, hormones are stimulated earlier. Some children are experiencing puberty from as early as nine or 10 years of age. In girls, breasts will bud, and in both genders pubic hair appears. Girls experience menarche, their first menstrual cycle, about two years after puberty begins.

Besides the factors mentioned above, family trauma, insecurity, abuse and violence can also influence children to reach puberty earlier. Children with settled families and secure environments appear to have extended childhoods. Early puberty can lead to early sexual activity and whereas this was generally a factor in adolescence, children as young as 11 are now engaged in sexual activity. And it is often the case that precocious girls attract the attention of older boys. It is a complex issue but one which needs to be understood and responded to with sensitivity and open communication (Epstein, 2019).

Your child might be one of the lucky ones who navigates the passage from childhood to adolescence with unruffled calm and you will be blessed if they do. But as you see from the above, this is not the case for all children.

Peer influences become stronger in the tween years and can be positive or negative. Your youngsters are also exposed to online influences like inappropriate pornography and may be prey to increasing cyber bullying. Because this bullying is impersonal and remote, it can be more vicious than the bullying that happens face to face.

> *'Mortals are easily tempted to pinch the life out of their neighbour's buzzing glory and think that such killing is no murder.'*
> **George Eliot, Middlemarch**

It's important to be aware of what is happening in older kids' school and social lives. You obviously can't monitor them all the time, but keep your feelers out for changes in behaviour, mood swings, changing eating habits and other unusual behaviours.

This age, like the later adolescent years, are when kids test the limits in a variety of ways. Because you are family and they can usually rely on the fact that you love them, paradoxically you might be the object of their worst behaviours. You might endure temper tantrums and outbursts when they're not allowed to do exactly what they want, where and when and with whom they want.

Laying out this rather negative picture is just a way of saying that communicating with tweens and teens, resourcing positive activity and creating security in their lives is vitally important. Despite all the changes they are going through and their apparent desire for independence, it's important that they know you're there to support and listen to them if they need it.

From nine years onwards, children's logical reasoning is increasing, but they are still unable to truly project the consequences of their actions. Just as you set boundaries when children were learning to walk, boundaries are important at this age.

According to the authors of *The Origins of You* (Belsky, Caspi, Moffitt, & Poulton, 2020), the effects of peer pressure and negative influences from beyond the family can be mitigated through care. Knowing where children are, who they are with and what they are doing is important. And this will continue to be the case as they enter adolescence which is a continuation of the factors I have introduced in this chapter.

Supporting communication

It is rare these days for families to share meals around a table. Perhaps the experience of COVID lockdown has made this more possible because people have been staying home, but in general the timetables of work, school, exercise and hobbies, makes it difficult for everyone to be home and seated at the same time. However, being around a table talking and listening, is one of the easiest ways to foster communication. Even if you only manage it a couple of times a week, finding topics to talk about, where everyone can offer their point of view is a great way for kids to learn about what their own values and beliefs are in life. Sharing conversation is made difficult if everyone is dialled into a device, so either exclude phones or ensure that the conversation continues around the checking in that everyone, even adults, seem to do these days. Some families have a basket in the middle of the table and everyone surrenders their device for the length of the meal.

When I reflect on my childhood, I am grateful for what was passed down during these conversations. My parents did so many things that influenced the education of my siblings and myself. Things besides sending us to school! They always saw themselves as the primary educators and never fully gave over the reins to anyone else.

If we came home with stories and information, they'd always add different perspectives. We'd crow, 'Anthony (fictitious name) was really naughty and didn't do his homework so he had to write lines.' They'd say, 'Maybe Anthony had to look after his little brothers yesterday, because both his mum and dad are working.' 'Oh. Yes. We didn't think of that,' we'd say. My father would often say, 'There, but for the grace of God, go you or I.' I am not affiliated with any organised religion, but this statement often comes to mind for me when I feel gratitude for all the remarkable gifts life brings each day.

Families are where so much good thinking and learning is grounded. It is during casual get togethers that your conversations will be salt and peppered with your family's interests, points of view and values. It is also a time to develop children's general knowledge. Because their world is expanding and they are party to news, social media and other wider influences, they'll benefit from having things explained to them. I remember how my siblings and I had conversations with my parents about wars, poverty, international terrorism, assassinations, natural disasters, murder and crime. Of course, all these things are disturbing. In your children's life span, many of these global influences are still at work and there is the addition of climate fear and the COVID pandemic to confront. My parents were able to handle the topics sensitively, to assure us that they were always looking out for us, and to put everything in perspective.

On the flip side, we also learnt about famous people, geography, sport, literature, poetry and film. We developed a great sense of humour and collected family anecdotes that we are now passing down to our own kids.

If they disagreed with something we experienced during our education, they would voice their opinions. And if we got into trouble at school they would support us without condoning what we'd done. We learned to suck it up if we'd crossed the line somewhere.

They actively gave us life education. I'm immensely grateful for a deep sense of belonging and the broad perspectives that operated in our home. Our parents live on in us every day. They weren't perfect, no parents are, but they were aware of seeding our future in every moment of every day.

Supporting emotional intelligence
At no time is emotional intelligence more important than in the years approaching adulthood. I mentioned earlier that whilst children between nine and 17 are developing complex intellectual abilities, they still have difficulty projecting consequences. Thinking through consequences is done in the prefrontal cortex of the brain and that is still under construction at this stage. In fact the process continues into the forties! What we often deal with in adolescence is the limbic system – the home of emotions. Self-esteem, self-image and self-worth are the areas that might be impacted. Your kids will find themselves somewhere on a spectrum from confident and happy to anxious and depressed. How do we support them to maintain a sense of balance during these tumultuous years?

I have already mentioned perspective taking as a thinking strength. When kids are aware that there is never only one way to look at things, they can shift their thinking and get themselves out of downward spirals. They can learn to evaluate where comments or opinions affecting them originate. They can assess whether the person, group or viewpoint is worth them experiencing hurt, negativity or rejection. As parents we can facilitate this ability. We can discuss how we deflect and discount things if they come from a source we don't respect or uphold. And only take seriously something that originates from a legitimate well-researched and unbiased source. (Hard to find in these days when even many journalists write to bolster opinions rather than thought.)

Older children are in a position to sort the wheat from the chaff in terms of validity, appropriateness and worthiness of attention. If they're in touch with their mental processes they will be aware that there are always alternatives. Being aware of alternatives provides an array of choices. Choices that relate to beliefs, experience and behaviours.

The difference between reaction and reflection
I like to frame this as a choice between reaction and reflection. We have all read about young people being involved in a king hit assault. This is often an unprovoked, unforeseen attack to the head which can and does maim or kill someone. Often the victim is left in a coma. I think these attacks are an extreme form of reactive behaviour. Any action where someone just acts out is reactive – there is no thought process to mitigate its outcome.

Reflection, on the other hand, provides a pause before the reaction to consider whether to go ahead. The pause can be infinitesimal, but it might change the course of someone's life. The ability to pause is an act of self-regulation which will be discussed in Part B of this book in more detail. The earlier individuals self-regulate their thoughts and behaviour, the more chance they have of life success (Belsky, Caspi, Moffitt, & Poulton, 2020).

Young people who act out at home may not always act out in the same way in public, but there is always the chance that they might. Talking with young people about noticing their emotions, understanding their thinking patterns and monitoring their emotional escalation can go a long way to ensuring their social interactions are more positive and successful.

Kids develop their sense of identity based on different things. Are your children identifying themselves as positive influences on the world, or do they cross over into a camp where they elevate themselves by belittling others? If they are doing the latter, it's worthwhile trying to trace the origins of that behaviour. They may be running with the wrong peer group.

Some kids at this age will be the target of bullies and they might need intervention. Only in families where there is open and honest communication might they even tell you about it. I hope they do. If you find out your children are being bullied, seek expert advice. In the past, parents might have just said 'Man up', even to the girls! But modern research shows how trauma has a long tail, and bullying has a profound effect on a person's sense of worthiness and sense of self-control.

Understanding their own emotions, being able to perceive others' emotions and having the ability to hit the pause button to reflect before reacting will go a long way to establishing and maintaining kids' meaningful, rewarding relationships.

Supporting school learning
You might ask, why it's important to focus on adolescent school learning? Surely to goodness it must be up to them by now? Part of the answer is that their ability and style of communication is the sum of what they hold in their brains. They, like us, can only consider and use what they know, so the more they know, the more they're able to problem-solve, launch creativity and engage with the world. Knowledge adds to personal mastery, a special level of proficiency in every aspect of life, personal and professional identity. In the book,

The Fifth Discipline, Peter Senge describes people with self-mastery as operating purposefully towards a vision based on their dynamic interaction with their own values and ideas. They are motivated, see their current situation as part of a journey and have a deep sense of connection. They know they will contribute to society. Having a purpose drives them to be creative in following their goals and engaging with others without sacrificing their own strong identity. They know that they will need to continue learning and despite that, they have deep self-confidence to step into the future (Senge, 2006).

These are high aspirations, but every person can develop their self-mastery.

Unlike the junior primary years, your adolescent children are unlikely to want you to get involved in their actual schoolwork except perhaps to help them resource projects. But what you can do is ensure they develop great study skills.

Sharpening study skills
I love the work of Tony and Barry Buzan. Tony Buzan, the inventor of Mind Maps®, has undertaken research in the areas of psychology, neurophysiology of the brain, semantics, memory and creative thinking. Based on his clinical research and case studies as a psychologist, he and his brother, Barry, present a list that positively influences learning and memory. Share this information with your kids. And give them large sheets of paper, coloured pens and sticky notes!

Buzan and Buzan outline six factors – perhaps you can try to memorise them as they are presented!

- The primacy effect – items from the beginning of the learning period are more easily remembered
- The recency effect – items from the end of the learning period are remembered more readily

- Association – any items associated with things or patterns already stored in the long-term memory are more easily connected and learned
- Emphasis – any items which stand out as being in some way remarkable or unique arrest attention because of their novelty
- Engaging the senses – any items which appeal particularly strongly to any of the five senses dwell in the memory for longer than usual impressions
- Individual interests – those items of particular interest to the learner will be more easily learned

A final extremely important thing about learning and memory is that it is best acquired when the learning is active. Based on the information above, there are some things you can do to support learning and we discuss these below.

Provide the right fuel
This is not part of the Buzan advice, but it is highly recommended to watch what children eat and drink (Medina, 2014). Composed of 80% water, the brain needs hydration to function! Sugary drinks and salty snacks induce brain fog, impair memory and lower concentration. Float raspberries or sliced strawberries in the tumbler. The fruits subtly flavour and flush toxins. Besides, who wouldn't eat the berries?

Colourful foods add zing to vitamin rich intake. Sliced fruit wins over whole fruit. Offer tiny bowls of raw nuts, sultanas, sliced banana and squares of anchovy toast. When you make the family spag bog, disguise the kale, spinach and broccoli in rich tomato sauce! I won't tell.

Routine
Time management is key. Support your kids to program things at the same time each day to engrain habits. Advise them to schedule regular breaks. It is proven that working in shorter blocks, perhaps 40 minutes at a time with mini breaks is more productive than working for long

stretches. This is because they study or work in shorter blocks and the primary and recency effects are more efficient. Also, their concentration will last for the whole session.

Focus

Focus is necessary for learning. No attention – no outcome. Attention is an acquired skill and it's worth monitoring how your children approach tasks. Do they jump in before understanding the question? Do they distinguish what is relevant and irrelevant? Can they plan and sequence the steps correctly? These skills are seldom explicitly taught at school, so you have an ideal opportunity to influence good problem-solving. Ensure they concentrate on one thing at a time. Multi-tasking doesn't work, (yes, it is proven!) so don't have a TV, music or other interference in the background (Horvath, 2019).

Memory must-dos

Using more senses engages more areas of the brain and enhances learning. For example, walking in the garden while reading sends more blood to your brain. As kids learn, encourage them to create mnemonics. When they have five things to remember, teach them to choose a key word from each and make a sentence. This works better than acronyms with first letters, because words are better cues. The sentence holds the information together and each word acts as a hook to retrieve the parts. This helps them to recall all the relevant information when required. Representing ideas with colourful pictures and diagrams also facilitates memory.

Practice and review

Encourage practice. Repeating tasks bulks up neurons. If you read the first chapter, you will recall myelin, a white fatty substance, laid down on the long part (axon) of the neuron which speeds up and improves learning networks. Practice grows the brain! Once kids know their work well, suggest they interleave the questions from different areas. If they know their times tables well, get them to skip around and do the 12 mixed with the eight. If they have mastered their arithmetic, interleave multiplication with the other operations. Each time they embark on a different type of task, their brain reboots. This is wonderful practice for when they hit the desk during tests and exams! Finally regular review of work makes it more sustainable. Before they start each day's task, encourage them to briefly revise what happened the day before.

Variety and challenge
After establishing good habits and routines, shake it up occasionally with variety and challenge! For tweens, prepare ahead but announce what seems a spur of the moment decision to do everything in the park, or at a picnic table outdoors. Challenges always motivate. Can they read more chapters than they did last week? Can they embark on their homework as a mission following a trail of clues with a reward at the end? Hopefully, a reward so worthwhile that next time you declare 'Mission Arithmetic', they jump to attention!

Arranging the environment

As mentioned earlier, privacy becomes an issue at this time. So, setting up older kids' spaces is important and it can be great fun. I remember being allowed to collect empty *Beechies* chewing gum packs to arranging around my room along the picture skirting. I also had posters of favourite pop groups on the cupboard doors. For the first time, we were allowed to choose our own bedding and arrange our furniture the way we wanted.

I shared a bedroom with my sister, but we each had our own allocated space and a small study area with our own homework and art implements. Organised space and personal work zones are motivating. Help kids embellish tins with bright paper for their writing utensils. A decorated carton, set on its side, makes a great bookcase and keeps things neat. Individualised space imprints identity, promotes competence and induces calm.

Part of getting on well with tweens is giving them control over their time. If you want them to achieve certain tasks or complete chores, set up a timetable for the family with each person's roles and commitments. When the expectations are agreed and scheduled, everyone will find it easier to do what's needed without continuous nagging. And get them to do chores like caring for the pets. We have two Tonkinese, Jasper and Mink, each with his own feline personality. The more kids do for themselves and for others, the better – as you will have read earlier!

Control over time and space in the home goes a long way to creating positive vibes.

Activities, outings and practical ideas

Family interests and extra-curricular activities

On top of having long conversations with our parents my siblings and I also had stories read to us at night, played board games and cards, were allowed to listen to one radio program just after lights out, listened to music, were taken to theatre, music and sport. We had dance and music lessons and had materials to paint and draw regularly. We did crossword puzzles on weekend afternoons. We were given chores, helped in the garden, had friends over and had picnics. Our parents belonged to service clubs and we'd turn up to help out when they were cooking, organising or hosting events.

When we visited relatives, we were encouraged to recite a poem, play a tune on the piano, or demonstrate something else we were learning. I am sure this early ability to stand and deliver set each of us up with confidence in public speaking and developed our leaderships skills.

Both parents patiently watched all our made-up gymnastics displays and concerts. They showed interest when we turned up to share what we'd learned, made, coloured or cooked. I know now that their interest in our planning, collaboration, activity, memory training and motivation was instrumental in developing our creativity.

As a continuation of developing children's interests and creativity discussed in relation to primary school children, give adolescents opportunities to strengthen their knowledge and expertise in areas they have already spent time on. It would be great if they could take their expertise out into the neighbourhood and share their skills with others. Starting a magic club, a chess tournament at school, a sewing circle for underprivileged children or tutoring will give your teens a great sense of purpose.

Make your home a popular gathering zone

One of the ways to sustain ties during the tween and adolescent years is to make your home an inviting place for your kids' friends to visit. Involve them all in cooking and preparing meals. In my experience the more you invite kids to help you, the easier it is to talk to them. Taking an interest in friends and getting to know their parents enables you to assess the tone and type of social interaction your children are engaging in. Plus, friends bring a vibrant atmosphere to homes and you will hear more about their shenanigans when they tease each other. Include friends in family outings to picnics, movies, the beach, agricultural shows, sports' matches, and attractions like the zoo or nature parks. This has the double advantage of engendering new interests in your own children and strengthening their social skills and friendships. Plus, your kids will become experts at the BBQ!

Encourage teens to look outwards to community

My experience of young people today is that they are more aware of the plight of others. They seem to be born leaders with great organisational skills. When your children support others, manage clubs or lead teams, they are contributing to society. When they work with others and learn about the experience of others, there is no doubt they develop more empathy and understanding.

Develop financial literacy

Your children learn a lot at school, but something that's missing from most curricula, unless your child studies business specifically, is financial literacy. If you are not up to speed with this yourself, it is worth encouraging your children to read books related to the topic or speak to someone in your network that can give them ideas about how to become financially viable citizens. This might start with advice not to get into debt, at a base level, but there are so many ways your children can learn to manage and make money. The book, *Rich Dad Poor Dad* by Robert T. Kiyosaki, is a great starter. Also*, Think and Grow Rich* by Napoleon Hill. And for more invaluable advice: Scott Pape's *The Barefoot Investor* and *The Barefoot Investor for Families: How to Teach your Kids the Value of a Buck*. And one final recommended book is financial journalist, Annabelle Williams' book, *Why Women are Poorer Than Men*. It is an eye-opening, research based and very scholarly piece of writing.

The majority of people miss out on opportunities to improve their lives and lifestyles because they are uniformed about money and how it works. The kind of information in these books could radically change your children's life trajectories, and even your own.

As difficult as tweens and teens might be, they are also an absolute delight to have around, often displaying a zany sense of humour and introducing us to the next stage of how the world will be.

I love this quote from Guilty Chocoholic Mama. I think it is a great way to view this time by not focusing on problems that might emerge, but rather on the great privilege it is to be around vibrant, amazing young people.

> *I don't just want to get through the teenage years. I want to cherish these years when my children are still living under my roof and sleeping in their beds and eating my food. I want to store up memories. I want to see stories come full circle. I want to have deep conversations. I want to honour big moments. I want to*

appreciate ordinary days. I want to celebrate accomplishments no-one else sees. I want to look back with gratitude and forward with hope. I want to know I did not take the gift of these years for granted. Because the love I have for my teens is not something I have to get through; it's something I'm holding onto.

IN SUMMARY:

- The tweens and adolescence are years of rapid change that can bring turmoil and confusion
- The world of older children expands to include peer and internet influences
- Puberty brings physical and emotional changes
- Be alert for changes in behaviour that might indicate problems being encountered
- Offer a safe, communicative environment but respect the wish for privacy
- Encourage independence but keep updated about where, when and with whom your children are spending time
- Encourage customisation of their space and independence to manage their time
- Make expectations clear and roster scheduled activities, chores and tasks
- Support your child's learning by teaching them the value of good study skills and mnemonics
- Ensure you children develop financial literacy because it will change the trajectory of their lives.

PART B

Wings

CHAPTER SIX

Taking Flight

'You will teach them to fly, but they will not fly your flight. You will teach them to dream, but they will not dream your dream. You will teach them to live, but they will not live your life. Nevertheless, in every flight, in every life, in every dream, the print of the way you taught them will remain.'
Mother Theresa

To begin this second part of the book let's return to Maslow's hierarchy of needs. I think you'll agree that in a family with mettle, children's hierarchical needs of food to survive, a safe nurturing environment, love, connection and a positive sense of self are met. In Part A, I concentrated on information, strategies and ideas you can enact to develop children's attachment, language, conceptual understanding, thinking and emotional intelligence. The motif throughout has been that having an excellent knowledge base, exercising different modes of thinking, acquiring a variety of skills and having articulate speech all support an individual's confidence and competence. Having confidence and competence are great pillars for resilience. They provide children and young people with the ability to bounce back, and the perseverance to stick to things for the long haul.

Everything discussed in Part A forms the basis of your children's ability to self-actualise – to spread their wings. However, when your offspring start to self-actualise, you may not find it as rewarding and predictable as you thought! And I warned you about that in the introduction. They might take off in a direction you never anticipated and even highly disapprove of! But be patient. You can't learn their life lessons for them. You can only attempt to make their journey less dangerous. And you might learn some truly remarkable life lessons from them.

Armour plating your children

In this part of the book, I want to focus on more philosophical aspects of building cohesion within families. As mentioned before, every family is unique and you may be a single, divorced, same sex, foster, adoptive parent or guardian. Human beings have invented and devised an immense variety of care relationships to nurture children and young people meaning that families are multi-faceted and blended in many ways. Cohesion engenders a sense of belonging. Belonging strengthens the ability to live through times of trouble. It helps the family stay solid despite difficulties and is highly necessary because no-one can dodge all life's bullets.

Our family emigrated from South Africa to Australia in 1998. This wasn't an easy decision because we left parents, relatives and very special friends behind to risk making a new life on a different continent.

On the day we left, we popped in to say goodbye to my mum. My son, Sean, then 10 years old, tripped running back to the car. He sliced his hand on a stone and we had a desperate rush to find a pharmacist at the airport to bandage him for the journey. I still have the vision of holding Sean's hand, walking beside my husband, Pierre, and watching five-year-old Candice ahead of us in an orange floral pant suit determinedly dragging her bag towards the plane and a blind future. She never forgave me for the poor taste of that outfit, and I still teasingly scold her for bringing contraband into Australia. When we arrived at the home of friends in Perth, I casually ran my fingers through Candi's hair and found a great big fat African grey tick attached to her scalp!

We brought with us many aspects of our old life and now, in the present, we continue to create new elements in our family identity even though our offspring are adults.

Prior to leaving South Africa we attended family counselling. The idea was to ensure we had the skills and were in a mental and emotional state of wellbeing strong enough to survive as a nuclear family and create a new life in a strange land. It's important to get professional input when it's needed.

Here are three important pieces of parenting wisdom I learned from the wisdom of psychologists:

1. Look after yourself first
As a parent the idea of looking after yourself first seems totally counterintuitive. Surely as parents or caregivers, it's our job to make sacrifices for our family? Yes, we do, but if you don't look after your own sanity and wellbeing and your own health, there is no way you'll have the energy to support anyone else. Candice once said to me, 'Mum, you're always there for everyone.' My answer was that I could only do it because I made time for me. I know that in global terms having a relaxing bath every day is an extreme luxury. But it is my respite and think tank.

Exercise is also important. Throughout my adult life, I have always done exercise. Be it aerobics, (yes, a' la' Jane Fonda in Lycra and legwarmers), competitive racewalking, cycling, Pilates, skiing, or golf, I have always loved the physicality of exercise. Most of my creative ideas and plans have been hatched pounding the roads with my headphones belting out very loud pop, reggae and R&B music. Eating relatively well, (no-one is a saint and I love chocolate) has also been habitual for decades. Because I make time for me, I don't feel resentful when I do things for someone else.

Self-care is important and there is research to prove it! Self-care contributes to your wellbeing and, by extension, benefits your child. Nim Tottenham, a professor of psychology at Columbia University who focuses on the interplay between caregiving and brain development, emphasises that we care for children by caring for parents. She says:

> *Parents ask me, 'What is the best parenting advice you can offer?' I tell them, 'Do what you can to take care of your wellbeing, to make sure you are feeling safe, and to manage your own emotions in a healthy way. When you feel this way, that gets translated to your children in a powerful way.'*

2. Use film and story to help formulate your children's thinking
When I discussed discipline and behaviour with our counsellor, she said that the world had created great ways to teach ethics, morality, courage and honour. The world had stories. She advised me to read heroic stories and introduce the kids to movies that were peopled with heroic, honourable characters. She suggested the *Iliad* and *Odyssey*, and I confess to never reading those classics, but story and film have always been important in our family for framing ideas and exploring values. Plus, this exposure helped to develop our off-beat brand of humour! There is more about the value of stories in a later section.

3. You are not your children's behaviour

The third important idea I still find valuable is to separate yourself from your kids' behaviour. You are not responsible for it. You should neither gloat nor feel guilty. They did it. Whether it's good or bad, they need to own it. You can engage with them about it, appreciate or abhor it, but dissociate yourself from it. At times in my life, this has been very difficult to do. But it has also helped me to keep a sense of perspective.

Forging a family identity

So, what are the ways to forge a family with mettle … a family that is coherent, resilient and strong?

Relational trust

It's hard to journey with someone you don't trust. No-one is perfect. Pierre and I are not perfect parents. But we do have a deep, abiding respect for one another. We appreciate and are grateful to share our lives. In Kahlil Gibran's thoughts on marriage, he says:

> *Stand together yet not too near together:*
> *For the pillars of the temple stand apart,*
> *And the oak tree and the cypress grow not in each other's shadow.*

As life partners, we have both grown. We've developed separate and combined interests. We check in often on each other's thoughts and opinions. We've developed a friendship as well as a marriage. Of course, we disagree about things and there are times we are angry with each other. But surely that is a part of life everyone has to deal with.

Not everyone is compatible in marriage, and some marriages don't last the distance. Many marriages end in separation. Does this mean the end to respectful relationships? Even when relationships break down, it is important to think about the impact on children and to find the best solutions to support them in the new circumstances. In my own family and circle of friends I have witnessed both toxic and amicable break-ups. There are no easy answers.

Speaking with one voice

Before we look at children, we need to look at ourselves. Children are wily and if they detect a tiny chink in our resistance, they'll use it to their advantage. So, when you bring children into the world, it's good to create a unified voice with your co-carer/s. Co-carers may be spouses, partners, your own parent or another person interested in supporting your child's upbringing. Unity is agreeing about how to conduct family life.

It helps if you have the same values and aspirations for your child, and if you have the same view on boundaries and behaviour expectations. But even if you don't, you need to do all the arguing about it before you tell the kids what to do.

Children respond to clarity. That's not to say that, when they are old enough, you can't declare your different points of view, you can, but then explain how you have reached a compromise around those views in your decision about whatever is at hand. If you allow your children to set you against one another, you are on a hiding to nothing. Part of this unity is honesty. If you collude with a child against a partner or fellow carer, it will end badly.

Have high expectations for your children

As a parent you have untapped power to positively influence your child's thinking in a variety of ways. You may have heard of the *Pygmalion effect*. Research shows that human beings respond to what others expect from them. Your expectations and how you interface with your kids have long-term effects on how they think, relate to others and view themselves. Words are more than words. What you choose to say out loud, will shape your child's thinking, so why not use this to their advantage?

Your communication sets the tone for your relationships. Parents are known to talk to kids in a way they never would to other adults. Have you heard tirades similar to this: 'How many times do I have to tell you to look after your stuff! You're an idiot! You're so irresponsible. Do you know how much that blazer cost?' Now shift and imagine saying this to a friend or other adult. It's possible but unlikely you would use a tone like that! On my Facebook I often see this recurring post: 'What do teenagers need these days?' Most people say they need manners, a sense of gratitude or discipline. My response is they need respect. The same as everyone else.

A fabulous book to read about communicating with your children is *How to Talk So Kids Will Listen and Listen So Kids will Talk* by Adele Faber and Elaine Mazlish (Faber & Mazlish, 1980). Throughout the book, their advice is to engage with youngsters in a respectful way, to explain rather than complain and to use positive specific praise to motivate them.

Broad praise like 'you're such a good or clever child', is actually undermining. It's not possible for children to always live up to these generalisations and they may even stop risk-taking or avoid challenges in case they don't live up to your ideals. It is proven that many children labelled gifted give up trying new things when they hit their first hiccup. They don't try so they won't fail. High expectations are not asking your children to always act out an impossible ideal.

It's more beneficial to select something specific to praise that they can permanently own. 'You really got yourself organised for an early start today! Thanks, that made the morning run so smoothly.' Or 'Your homework today is neat and you were responsible to get it out of the way before dinner. Now you can go and watch that program you've been looking forward to.' Praising something and explaining why it's helpful gives kids a boost. The specific praise relates to a limited timeframe, so they don't feel like they have to act their whole life out according to a general expectation.

When you remonstrate with children, it's also important not to be general. Children often hear statements like 'You are always late', 'Your room is always a mess', 'You are never nice to your brother'. These blanket statements are demoralising and can have a lasting impact on children's self-esteem. View each of these behaviours as one-offs and limited. Explain why they need attention and work through strategies to improve behaviours over time. No-one wants to feel like they're a permanent loser. And be consistent when you do eke out consequences. If you allow your mood to determine the severity of the consequence, rather than agreed boundaries and consequences, your children will never know what's coming next resulting in anxiety, even fear.

Sibling rivalry, or sibling tribalry?
When Candice, was about eight or nine years old she was obsessed with Pokémon. So was Sean. They both collected and swapped cards with their friends. Candice was given a Pokédex for her birthday. It was her most treasured possession because she could look up any character and research its powers and stats. One day it simply vanished and believe me, there were tears!

About four years later, Sean got a notification that it was his school year's turn to retrieve a time capsule his class had 'buried' as a project when they were in Year Eight. Yes, you guessed it, out came Candi's Pokédex! I am not sure if she's forgiven him yet.

There were a few years when they absolutely did not get on. And I am sure that you find the same in your family. But if siblings can't get along and respect one another, you won't have a happy family dynamic. You'll never escape the teasing, practical jokes, odd hysterical screaming match or jealous tantrum. But underneath all that, the hope is that you will convince them to see the value of strong connections. As described earlier, we arrived in Australia as a nuclear family of four. We had to stress often the importance of having good ties and good relationships. As adults, my kids get on very well and confide in one other even though they currently reside in different cities.

My own siblings also live far away! We are in Australia, England and Spain. But we have a sibling call every week on a Saturday night Australia time. It is a combination of friendship, therapy, advice seeking and giving, congratulations, support and a good measure of irreverent laughter. We solve all the problems of the world once a week. It sustains us and we feel connected despite the tyranny of distance. We are a tribe of three.

If you want your children to be good siblings to one another, one of the ways to nurture their relationship is to not compare them to one another. I often hear parents say: 'Mandy is our scientist and James is our artist.' These comments pigeonhole your children and as mentioned before, they may suffer from the Pygmalion effect and live out your expectations. And don't let teachers get away with this either. A second child going into a teacher's domain does not want to hear about how wonderful, terrible, clever or unruly their sibling was before them!

Worse comparisons are, 'Anita was so brilliant at maths, I just don't understand how Emily missed out on those genes'! Or 'Anita is a little neat freak, and Emily – well, her room is a veritable floordrobe.' What must Emily think of herself?

Don't talk about your kids in front of them as though they aren't there and don't give your friends and acquaintances fuel to think negatively about your kids. They deserve confidentiality about their foibles. Of course, there are family members you totally trust and who may be helpful when you are at a loss with how to deal with one of your offspring but be absolutely sure of their confidentiality code when you share with them.

Another suggestion is not to feel as though if you buy one child something that you have to buy them all the same or an equivalent thing. Get them the things they need when they need them. If your son needs a cricket bat, so be it. If it's a daughter's birthday, let her enjoy the specialness of gifts on her own.

If you want them to be friends for life, don't set them up against each other in any way.

And spend time with each of your children on their own. They will love their special time with you.

Be open to listening to your children

In the same breath as I earlier spoke about developing unity with your partner, you need to be aware of not ganging up on your child. It's easy to do this if you don't listen carefully to what they have to say. Carla Rinaldi, the CEO of the Reggio Children describes listening as taking someone 'out of anonymity' (Rinaldi C. , 2001). In a sense, when someone listens carefully to understand your perspective, you experience yourself as a valued person. Pierre adds to this idea of listening and he enjoys posing open-ended questions. His belief is that open-ended questions will give you interesting and even surprising feedback!

I've been guilty of not listening many times! When Sean was about 14, he was passionate about video games. He asked us to get him a connection cord to plug in his device so it could charge it in the car when we were travelling. Our 'parental unit' as he calls us, thought he was spending too much time on games and we point blank refused. I feel really awful now about this blanket decision. It has taken me years to realise that his interest in games was part of the new world order. The honing of his identity as a digital native.

This was reiterated in Technicolor recently when I tried to operate a game as part of my interest in digital technology for children's education. I was utterly hopeless. I realised that my children had both developed phenomenal abilities to manipulate space and time concepts, to strategise through an infinite number of possible outcomes and had mastered future forward concepts. I had been left behind. They were both highly amused and said: 'Mum, you're worse than a baby!' And it's true.

There is clearly an issue with digital addiction in young people, but our stance in Sean's teens was short-sighted.

Think three in-between

In the anecdote above, as parents we displayed an either/or mentality. But we didn't always make decisions like that. When children make requests, it's helpful to think win-win, rather than win-lose. If we put our minds to it, we can usually come up with two or three alternatives. It is good to include the kids themselves in brainstorming workable solutions.

I often see children howling when they can't get what they want in a store or supermarket. This is avoidable if you have worked out a system with your children about receiving gifts and treats. There may be special times and days when the 'sometimes' food is available. And there may be ways to earn what they want you to buy for them.

In his teens, Sean desperately wanted an Xbox. Because he already owned a PlayStation, we couldn't see the benefits. Everything in the modern world seems to be freely available and disposable. Children are used to instant gratification. It can be hard to instil a value system of earning something you want, rather than being given it on a platter.

To earn the Xbox, Sean delivered newspapers. He usually did this on his bicycle. On occasions he'd just be exhausted and he'd ask me at 5.00am to drive him around his circuit. Because he was so dedicated, I didn't mind and actually enjoyed the time we spent together. On one such morning, he hurled a rolled paper onto a veranda and it broke a window beside the front door. He ran to my car mortified and begged me to go and speak to the owner. He stood at the gate as I gingerly knocked on the door. An outraged homeowner yanked it open saying, 'Did you see the paper boy?' I apologised and said, 'I own the paper boy.' Sean was able to apologise and I think the newsagent paid for the damage. The stories of Sean's newspaper delivery are part of family folklore. Once he lay down next to his bicycle at the side of the road and had a nap much to the consternation of a passer-by who stopped to check if he was okay. I also learned later that when a nasty woman yelled at him for not putting the paper into her post box, he dutifully did it thereafter, but always added a few snails for good measure!

Thinking of three in-between alternatives and compromises can go a long way to keep peace in a family. Sean got his Xbox and genuinely appreciated it.

Establishing boundaries

And what about discipline? Ab initio, as a parent you are not put on this earth to be your child's friend. Yes, of course there will be times when you are friends, but it is not your key role. As parents, guardians or carers, your role is to support children, tweens, teens and young adults to become socially responsible and achieve life success. Living together in society goes beyond the family. There is a tacit social contract and you are the one who sets the example of how to conduct family and communal life. This means that they can't always have their own way.

In the book *The Origins of You*, the authors discuss self-regulation as one of the most important qualities for future success (Belsky, Caspi, Moffitt, & Poulton, 2020). Included in the idea of self-regulation is the ability, as mentioned above, to delay gratification. Most achievements in life depend on this ability. You can't pass exams unless you jump study hurdles. You won't be an expert dancer without practice. You won't get fit without training. It's worth helping your children to develop planning and perseverance skills early on in life.

The Origins of You explores the multiple data collected in a longitudinal research study based on the Dunedin project in New Zealand. The study has followed a cohort of all the babies born in Dunedin between 1 April 1972 and 31 March 1973. One of the tests administered when children were three years of age is called the marshmallow test. In the test, children are given a marshmallow on a plate. They are told that the adult will return in a couple of minutes and if the marshmallow has not been eaten, they'll receive a second one.

Children have found ingenious ways to 'not eat' the treat including hiding from it, putting the whole thing in their mouth and then removing it, talking to it, blocking their eyes and ears, singing and turning their back on it. Some just can't resist and gobble it the instant the adult leaves. There is a great YouTube video (Flood San Diego, 2021) capturing how children devise strategies to earn the second marshmallow! Walter Mischel was the Stanford professor who originated the test and, in his book, *The Marshmallow Test – Mastering Self-Control*, he proves that early acquisition of the ability to delay gratification is a critical skill predicting more advanced educational outcomes, better social and thinking skills, a healthier lifestyle and commanding a better self-image (Mischel, 2015).

Delaying gratification and exercising self-control can be learned. Setting boundaries, time limits, having discussions about why you have rules and negotiating terms with children can go a long way to helping them develop these skills. And the earlier this is done the more effective the skills will be in enabling children to work towards goals and to become future orientated.

Of course, for the boundaries to be effective they need to reasonable and it is important to listen to your child and get their input into what is fair for their age, their social group and their interests. Part of learning to delay gratification is understanding the logic that underpins the rules or regimens you have in place. If homework is important to you, you need to explain why. If having a curfew is important, explain why. Work with your children on compromises that make sense to both of you. Do they need to extend their curfew because, in fact, it is safer for them to travel home with their friends, who have a later curfew? Or is your daughter or son the most responsible person in the party the others rely on to ensure they all keep safe?

Family meetings

In his book *7 Habits of Highly Effective Families*, Stephen Covey recommends developing a family mission statement. Whilst our family is aware of the values we share, we never went so far as to create a written mission statement. But when important things needed to be discussed we did and do still set a family meeting. The idea is to provide a space for everyone to speak and listen and to make decisions together. This has been helpful over the years to get over some of the bumps in the road.

When anxiety makes them spin out of control

I was driving to a weekend destination with my daughter who was on the brink of VCE (school ending) exams. She was in a flat spin. She thought the whole thing was too much for her. She was having a few social issues and had had a run-in with one of her teachers. She was threatening to throw in the towel.

I pulled into McDonalds' drive through and ordered a McChicken burger for each of us. (No, I don't do this every day!) Then I asked her to focus on one thing – to eat the burger.

Anxiety is often the result of catastrophising all the things that might happen in the future. It is a sense of being out of control.

As we ate, I told her about a day 10 years earlier when she had helped me. I'd been raging around the house in a state of panic because I had so much to do and absolutely no idea how I was going to achieve it. I was running an early learning centre, organising an exhibition, looking after a family and it was report time!

Candice was eight years old. She took my hand and moved me to my desk. She handed me a ruler, pencil and sheet of A3 paper. 'Make a plan mummy,' she said. 'Write down all your chores and make a time for them. You will do it if you think of one thing at a time.' It was a blessing. I did it and all the anxiety dissipated.

What Candice had happened on was simple mindfulness. To focus on the present. To use the current opportunity and not to be distressed about what might go wrong in the future. To prepare for the future one step at a time.

Every time I start to spin out, I think of this and calm down. I hope it can help you and your family too, to put everything into perspective.

When to outsource to experts

Children with illness, disabilities or trauma

Millions of families deal with the hardest of situations when their children are ill or experience levels of disability. No-one else walks in your shoes. If you are one of these families you will know more than me or anyone else how difficult it can be. It is my earnest wish that every family facing these issues will find the professional assistance and support they need to cope.

In the schools and infant-toddler centres in Reggio Emilia, these children are regarded as having 'special rights'. The educators operate from a culture of inclusion. It is worthwhile fighting for your child's inclusion and rightful place in the world around them.

Professor Reuven Feuerstein, the cognitive psychologist I have mentioned before, made a statement that initially shocked me. He said about a child: 'If you love me, do not accept me as I am.' Because we have acceptance literally hammered into us, I initially found the statement confronting. But he made the statement from a place of love. His meaning was that all children deserve the best support and education available for them to become as competent and participative as possible.

Professor Feuerstein was a brilliant scholar and a student of Jean Piaget in Geneva. After the second world war, he was tasked with the education of young survivors of the Holocaust. Some of these young people were so traumatised that they were elective mutes. The level of trauma they had suffered meant that they had to start, not from the beginning, but make up time and develop enough motivation to even reach the starting blocks. As he worked with them, designing tasks to engage their thinking and working toward building a sense of optimism for their future, he became aware that their brains were changing. It was in the days before brain plasticity was an accepted phenomenon, and he named what he was witnessing structural cognitive modifiability (SCM). He described SCM as a profound and permanent change of brain activity. In the 21st century we recognise SCM as plasticity. The ability of the brain to transform through a variety of stimulations and experiences is now well documented. What is clear is that persistent, professionally designed early intervention has long-term benefits for a wide variety of issues facing young children. It is worth seeking out the professionals who can provide the precise interventions that can assist your child to reach their unique potential.

Early, targeted intervention
It is often parents who first notice when some developmental milestone is not reached. A friend of mine's second child, a son, was well on his way to talking. After a few months, he seemed not to be progressing as much as she anticipated. She took him to several medical appointments and was told that children all developed their speech at different rates and she shouldn't be concerned, just patient. But one morning it struck her

that his speech had not only stopped progressing, but it also appeared to be reversing! He had lost the ability to pronounce syllables that he'd previously mastered. He had been able to say 'baboon' perfectly clearly, now he was just saying 'boon'. More determined than ever, she finally gained a referral to see an ear, nose and throat specialist. They discovered that his ears were completely impacted because of chronic infection. Once grommets were in place and the infective impaction subsided, his speech immediately improved. If she hadn't been persistent, her son may have had development delays for much longer.

At about four years of age, my own son was diagnosed with low muscle tone and I was informed that he needed occupational therapy for sensory integration. He was also diagnosed with attention deficit disorder (ADD). It's not easy receiving theses diagnoses, but now, when he is a high functioning adult, I am eternally grateful to the therapists and learning specialists who supported him during his early schooling.

A recent autism research study indicates that very early intervention, before the age of two years, can be game-changing. The intervention is done by the parents who are guided by specialists to recognise their infant's unique way of communicating. After close observation they are given techniques to enrich their child's language, expression and social engagements. This is reportedly one of the first pre-emptive studies, which reframes therapy from a 'wait and see' to an 'identify and act' approach. The objective of the study was to provide support systems before diagnosis which usually occurs at around age two. At age three the therapy had worked so well that the children did not qualify for an autism diagnosis and their communication and social skills were positively impacted. Called iBASIS-VIPP therapy, this study increased parental responsiveness to their child's unique communication and had significant positive effects (Whitehouse, Green, & Hudry, 2021).

Be it medical, physical, psychological or developmental, parents do not have all the knowledge and expertise to support their children when they are struggling. Trust your intuition and search for the people with the ability to support you.

Get support yourself when you need it!
It's not only children who may need support. Throughout my adult life, I've attended several rounds of counselling and relied on experts for advice. If you feel you need a helping hand, it's important to ask your GP or other health professionals where to exact the support that matches your requirements.

CHAPTER SEVEN

The Hard Conversations

'Flow like water around obstacles.'
Bruce Lee

No family will get through life without encountering obstacles. Bruce Lee famously said that we need to flow like water around obstacles. This thinking suggests nimbleness, flexibility and agility when approaching circumstances. But it's not easy. Flowing like water is not avoiding the obstacles, it's absorbing them into the stream of life and dealing with them. You can't leave someone on the bank as you flow on by! Part of mettle in a family is looking after everyone. Nine times out of ten, prevention is the best option, and future-proofing children is sometimes, if not always, attainable. So have the hard conversations. If things still happen, then deal with them as needed.

No family can avoid hard conversations. If you've established good communication channels from the start, they'll be easier than if you haven't. Communication by its definition is a two-way street. What many of us are not good at is listening. If your child feels like their experiences, emotions, points of view and desires are important to you and that you have given them fair consideration they will learn to trust and respect your judgement as you do theirs. You will have credit in the family trust bank.

Still, challenging conversations will arise. What I have found over time is that they are easier when we are not face to face! This seems counterintuitive.

The power of side-by-side conversations

When moving beside one another walking, or travelling in a car, the quality of communication is essentially different. Perhaps because the parties have to focus on two things, moving and the conversation, and because there is no direct eye contact, it seems easier to both deliver and receive messages. Also, you can give yourself time to think as you point something out or appear briefly distracted.

When walking outside, it is possible that the bilateral motion and higher oxygen levels energise our brains. Being outdoors may calm our emotions because the attention is broadened beyond the communication pair making it less confronting (Baum, 2018).

I have also had conversation with both my kids in a doorway! It seems the physical presence of an escape port allows for honest, inquiring and deep conversations.

Finally, conversations from a distance are a desperate saving grace. I've had long, hard conversations with Sean on the phone. On rare occasions when things boiled over, he fled the house and found a spot at an internet café to settle and calm his frayed nerves. My nerves also got a break! Then he'd open a conversation via text or email. These conversations were godsends because at least I knew my child was safe – and the distance gave us the space needed to nut out serious disagreements or conflicting points of view. Any contact is better than no contact. Do everything you can to keep in touch.

The worst period of time, and it can happen in all families, is when you lose communication completely. At one point, I confess to relying on Candice to be the conduit of news about her brother. Thankfully, these times were short-lived and we all now have flourishing relationships, but life is bumpy and life is hard.

When the sh*t hits the fan

Between now and end of this chapter, I present a series of the difficult issues which modern families face. I am not an expert in these. Part of the discussion is based on my personal experience of dealing with some of the problems and the advice psychologists and experts who helped me provided. And part of the information is from online research. Each family will deal with these issues in their own way, so writing about them here is more of an alert, than a recommended course of action.

Dealing with addiction
As stated earlier, no-one can dodge all life's bullets. There will be times when families are overcome by difficulties and life-changing events.

My family has experienced inter-generational addiction to alcohol and drugs. I have witnessed lying, subterfuge, theft, social withdrawal, dysfunctional family life, job losses, divorce, trouble with the law, imprisonment, domestic violence, motor accidents, personal injury, dislocation, homelessness, shortened lives and suicide related to addiction. On the bright side, I have also seen determination, renewal in self-belief, recovery, immense courage and personal thriving beyond addiction. The individual stories across three generations are not mine to tell. But there are some things I can attest to.

Do all you can to educate your family
If you can prevent your children from becoming addicted in the first place, you and they will be ahead of the curve. There is scientific evidence that substance abuse has long-term effects on cognition and emotion. At any age extensive drug and alcohol addiction is harmful, but it is particularly deleterious if it commences in adolescence.

Adolescent exposures to substances of abuse, such as alcohol, cannabis, and MDMA, cause persistent disruptions of cognition (Brown et al., 2000; O'Shea, McGregor, and Mallet, 2006; Piper and Meyer, 2004; Stiglick and Kalant, 1982). These findings indicate that the adolescent brain, which is still developing, is susceptible to insult from drug use and abuse, and such insult can result in long-lasting changes in affect and cognition (Gould, 2010).

Changes in affect and cognition can impact on planning, decision-making, lifestyle choices, career opportunities, social relationships and financial stability (Belsky, Caspi, Moffitt, & Poulton, 2020).

Addiction occurs in two stages.

The first stage occurs when a substance disrupts and deregulates the reward system in the brain. The reward system usually supports and responds to life-sustaining activities like eating and procreation. Drugs of abuse over-activate this system triggering 'abrupt and large increases in N-acetyl cysteine (NAC) dopamine' signaling intense pleasurable sensations.

The substance induced 'high' motivates the user to repetition of the experience. The reward centre is hijacked from life sustenance to substance ingestion. But over time it takes more of the substance to access the same high.

The second stage of the addiction is when early withdrawal symptoms occur and the user becomes vulnerable to relapse. The crucial cognitive areas impacted relate to decision-making, long and short-term memory and identity. If the use continues the drugs have the capacity to act on declarative memory, that part of the memory that defines individuals. And underperformance of declarative memory has potentially far-reaching negative effects. The cognitive debilitation affects the brain's ability for long-term abstinence, so a cycle of abuse is habituated.

Drugs
I smoked for eight years from 17–25 and although I have been teetotal for more than 10 years, I used to enjoy lovely glasses of mostly white wine. I loved a Chardonnay. But I was never tempted to smoke marijuana or take other drugs. My parents continually educated our family about the possibility of becoming addicted after a single episode and talked regularly about the effects of drug taking. But I don't think my avoidance was from their input alone. When I was about 14, we had a young police officer visit our school.

He showed us the different varieties of drugs, and we were able to smell and handle the samples. He showed us the 'pretty pills', the grass, the vials and hypodermics. He outlined the stages of addiction and how our behaviour might be influenced. He talked us through the modus operandi of drug dealers. First you get something for free from people who profess to be your friend. Once you get into the racket, they start to charge you for the substance. If you can't pay, there are other things you can do for them. This includes sexual favours, petty theft, shoplifting, stealing from your own family and helping them to sell more drugs. Then when you can't or won't deliver, they start to threaten your physical safety and they might stretch to threaten your family.

Potential diseases like Hepatitis C were described. (Since my schooling there is of course the threat of spreading HIV when needles are shared or drug preparation is unhygienic.) Then he presented three real life case studies of kids just like us, who had been caught in the trap. One was in jail and two, a young woman and young man, were dead. One was murdered and the other suicided. I knew the boy who had suicided, Bradley (false name), the eldest son of our next-door neighbours.

This real life 'education' put me in a much fuller picture. And I was able to pick up on the signs when I was later exposed to dealers at dance clubs, at senior school and at university. Drug distribution in Australia is big business and it's extremely sophisticated. In recent years, the dangers have spread from cities into country towns. A physician on the Mornington Peninsula, Victoria, in 2021 attests that drug related issues form by far the greatest number of his cases.

Don't think your kids are immune from all this, they are the target of all this.

Alcohol
Alcohol is another matter. Alcohol is legal. It is socially acceptable and easily obtainable. Indeed, there is a full-blown culture of alcohol consumption. If you don't drink, or don't drink as much as your friends do, or at as early an age as them, you may be branded 'uncool'. There is a kind of heroic aura about having a blinder. I was truly horrified when on talk-back radio one afternoon, a young woman in her late teens called in to say she wore her driver's licence around her neck as 'bling' so when she passed out, someone would be able to give a taxi driver her address to get her home. And this is a great segue, to promising your children that you will collect them from anywhere, anytime, no questions asked if they need you to! Do it. Go get them anytime – from anywhere!

Most teenagers will get through the stage when, off their face, they're being scraped off the sidewalk. But many don't, many become alcoholics.

And the long-term effects of alcohol are as significant as those for illegal drugs.

So, what can you do?

Don't normalise alcohol or drugs for children

There was a powerful advert on Australian television showing a typical backyard BBQ. A dad was with his mates and calls over his four-year old son, saying 'Maty, go get me another ale from the fridge, hey.' Far out, get your own darn drinks! If you do have the urge to overindulge occasionally, try and not do it in front of your kids! Children learn much, much more from observing our behaviour than from any words that come out of our mouths. Have frank discussions with your children about this issue and do it regularly. It's helpful if family discussion is already a key part of your family life.

Keep tabs on peer group activity

From nine years onwards, peers begin to exert more influence on your children than you do. This is part of growing up and it's a healthy development. It can work in a positive way and your kids can become interested in common hobbies, sports or cultural events. It can equally be negative where children learn new behaviours and participate in socially unacceptable, deleterious or even illegal activity.

A friend of mine had a foster son. They had an excellent relationship until he was 12. Then he became secretive and defensive, even aggressive in how he communicated with her. She realised he was leaving the house at night. He had got himself involved with a group of young men whose nocturnal activity included tagging the urban landscape with graffiti, upturning dustbins, shoplifting, drinking and drug peddling. It was heartbreaking for her. Fortunately, with the help of a counsellor and a teacher mentor at his school he turned his behaviour around and he is now married and holds down a regular job. If she didn't step in and seek professional aid to divert his path, the scenario may have been very different.

Recognise the signals

When kids are addicted, they have behaviour changes. They might be moody, less socially engaged with family, go out with unfamiliar friends and be out of contact. If their addiction is advanced, they might lie, steal and even threaten their siblings. Sometimes, if you're really lucky one of their friends, or friends' parents will alert you. You have to be honest with yourself when you notice these things, because your kid needs help! Overcoming addiction is generally not achievable by an individual on their own. Cold turkey is overrated. People literally need re-education and rehabilitation.

Interventions

If your child is addicted to narcotics or alcohol, and you can't talk them into getting treatment, intervene. If you look the other way, you enable the behaviour. The fall into addiction has stages. The earlier you catch it, the more likely it is that they'll recover and recommence a normal productive life. In the 1940s a Yale physiologist Elvin Morton Jellinek, analysed the surveys of thousands of alcohol addicts and discovered that there were trends within the data. He isolated several stages on an addiction curve. Whilst the work was initially only related to alcohol addiction it was also found to be relevant to other forms of addiction (Vertava Health, 2021).

Stages of the Jellinek Curve

Stage one: Pre-Alcoholic – drinking commences socially, but some drinkers find relief from stress and tension while imbibing.

Stage two: Prodromal (early alcoholic) – there is an escalation and preoccupation with drinking. Guilt may be associated with consumption and there may be attempts to hide it. There may be blackouts and episodes of extreme drinking, but the behaviour may not be detected as alcoholism.

Stage three: The Crucial Phase (middle alcoholic) – there is a loss of control around consumption and social and work issues may become impacted. Even if there is temporary abstinence, the battle is lost and drinking resumes. Friendships, family life and health are impacted.

Stage Four: Chronic Phase (late alcoholic) – there are benders, involving prolonged bouts of drinking. These lead to impaired thinking or even psychotic episodes. Despite not feeling psychological relief from drinking, the addiction is so high that the individual is unable to stop. Cold turkey stoppage could actually lead to life-threatening withdrawal symptoms.

Rock Bottom: Whilst Jellinek himself did not include this stage; the bottom of the curve is usually described this way. If people aren't supported out of the curve, they can cycle around at the bottom quite literally until they die from addictive disease.

But there is an upward side of the curve called the path of recovery.

The sooner on the downward curve the upward path of recovery can commence the less permanent is the damage from addiction. Often families wait until the 'hit rock bottom' stage, when a young person finds themselves in deep trouble in ways described above.

Treatment and recovery
Drug and alcohol recovery organisations can help with interventions and get kids into programs. Alcoholics Anonymous (AA) treats recovering addicts using a Twelve Steps program. Narconon supports addicts of narcotics and also provides services for families. Cognitive Behaviour Therapy (CBT), counselling, retreats, halfway houses, out-patient care are different formats for dealing with the issues. There are private and state clinics specialising in assisting young people to get their lives and their minds back. At no time, in all this discussion am I suggesting these truths and processes are easy. But if you love your child, you will go through the hoops.

Unconditional love
Even if kids are on the straight and narrow, there will be days you dislike them! When young people are in deep trouble with addiction, you might honestly want to turn your back and wash your hands of them. But this is when they need your support the most. When they are living through rewiring their brains and redefining their personal identities, they will not be very lovable. As Pierre says, sometimes unconditional love is the hardest kind. It doesn't mean giving them what they want, but often the exact opposite. Unconditional love can be tough love. But just do it. Love them.

Look after yourself
Most good programs for addiction include family counselling. You may be invited into a child's session or be offered counselling specifically for yourself. It is well worth attending. Besides feeling better, you will become educated about what the addicted young, or older, person is going through. You will also learn a heap of survival strategies.

I don't want to leave this section without talking about two more areas of addiction affecting the population including young people: gambling and pornography.

Gambling
Gambling has always impacted families, and in Australia it seems you cannot turn a corner without having access to it in some form or another. This has worsened with the advent of online gambling. Because it is so accessible and easy, there is no distance between the idea and the action. Added to accessibility, the billions being invested in online advertising is literally mindboggling. Take note how pervasive gambling advertising is during prime-time broadcasting. Like me, I'm sure you're aghast not only by how many sports betting adverts are interspersed between the news announcements, but also that the people in the adverts are all young. There was an ad recently where a person used one of those maddening, unsolicited calls from a call centre as an excuse to leave a family dinner table to place telephone bets.

Why is this an issue? Because it ruins lives and livelihoods. Like the other addictions, it increases over time and people get sucked in deeper and deeper. A friend I worked with got pulled into the gambling wormhole and lost the home she'd spent years saving for. It was utterly tragic. I'm not against the odd bet on special occasions, or spending a limited, planned amount on entertainment, but like the odd drink, or joint, the habits can turn into addiction and as carers, parents and responsible adults we can actively deter youngsters from becoming involved.

In 2018 it was reported that young people are committing suicide related to gambling addictions. A young man, name withheld here, thought he had won AU$30,000, but when he tried to claim it, the company told him that he'd won the sum in online credits. They took his real money but would not pay out real money. The shock and disappointment drove him to suicide (News.com.au, 2019). Several international research studies have shown that people with problem gambling are at a higher risk of suicide attempts and actual suicide. A Glasgow study estimates that addicted gamblers are nine times more likely than other youths, to attempt suicide.

Pornography

Imagine my horror when I opened my iPad one afternoon before legislation prevented pop-up ads, and an unsolicited pornography site invaded my consciousness. It featured schoolgirl models in poses inviting anal sex. The girls were so young it shredded my heart. I felt utterly nauseated. How had these young women been persuaded to pose for these photographs? I may sound like your Aunty Hilda about this. I respect that many women choose a career related to human sexuality and that is 100% their right. What needs to be the focus is whether exploitation at any level was involved in the creation of these online images. The Australian program *The Hunting* (IMDb, 2019) explores this issue in terms of the upload of images freely sent but uploaded without the permission of the person who either took their own photos or gave permission to be photographed.

It is reported that almost 50% of young people between nine and 16 years of age are regularly exposed to sexual images (AFP, 2020). Also, that these images shape practices which may be associated with unsafe sexual health such as omitting to use protection and engaging in unsafe anal and vaginal sex. The pornography often depicts violence and domination. The depictions can create expectations that young people should not regard as 'the done thing'. I'm not suggesting that every teenager who views pornography is going to suffer outcomes like this, but they do need to be aware of the risks. One way to counteract the impact of widespread pornography is open, honest communication. Discussion about the role of sex in relationships, the kinds, the expectations and dignity of making choices which are comfortable may go some way to helping young people navigate this essential relationship-based activity of life. These sorts of issues were among those discussed in the car with a kid in the back seat! But they needed to be had.

Safe sex
Clearly safe sex is an important issue to guard against sexually transmitted diseases and avoid unwanted pregnancies. If this conversation is beyond you, the lack of information or poor information can be overcome by offering your kids books on the subject or suggest some of the friendly, respectful but informative websites for young people on the topic. A conversation needs to be had about anal sex. Not from a moral, but from a physiological perspective. There is a possibility of spreading bacteria and damage to the sphincter because there is no natural lubrication in the area (Nall, 2019) (Markland, Dunivan, Vaugan, & Rogers, 2016). For teenagers who do engage in anal sex, there is sound practical advice available (FACT Dr, 2021) (Terlizzi, 2021).

Grooming
The digital world has moved too fast for parents and many of them don't understand how their kids are being targeted online. They underestimate the disastrous consequences of digital predation on young people.

Young people today are digital natives. They appear linked to the internet by a virtual umbilical cord. We are all aware, that every modern invention has a good and bad side. So, as wonderful as Facebook, Instagram, Twitter and other platforms are for social connection, they are equally capable of being used for social manipulation, bullying and predation. Education about the methodology of online predators is crucially important.

Kids love having digital followers. To acquire the following, they might decide to keep their profiles public. This makes them visible to literally anyone in the world including hackers, groomers, criminals and voyeurs. The daughter of a close acquaintance of mine was inveigled into an online 'romance' that cost her in excess of $10,000 because she was tricked into funding false cancer treatment for her online 'beau'. He presented himself as an ex-serviceman in the US army who had supposedly participated in operations in Afghanistan. Over a period of months virtually everything she earned from her part-time job went into a foreign bank account. It was discovered that the scam originated out of Bulgaria and the perpetrator was predictably catfishing. The settings are available to keep your profile private and kids are better off limiting who can access theirs.

There are also situations where young women are lured into relationships, filmed and then blackmailed by their so-called boyfriends. And of course, there are situations where young people are ambushed and assaulted.

In a report from the Australian Federal Police (AFP) research found that despite 'just under 17,000 reports of online child sexual exploitation received by the ACCCE in 2019, the Australian-first research found only 21% of parents and carers think there is a likelihood that online child sexual exploitation can happen to their child' (AFP, 2020). It is reported in the same research study that 'four out of five children aged four are using the internet; 30% of these children have access to their own device' and 'only 51% of the research participants sit with the children while they use the internet'.

The AFP works in partnership with the Commonwealth Bank of Australia, Datacom and Microsoft on an initiative called ThinkUKnow (Think U Know, 2021) which curates excellent resources for parents and educators with strategies to prevent children becoming targets or victims of online predation. The AFP also works with State and Territory Police on this initiative and it is well worth checking the advice on this platform.

Two final comments on the impact of digital platforms are worth mentioning. What young people post online doesn't ever go away. It is almost impossible to delete or erase things that have left a device. Prospective employers are now using these platforms to check on and assess potential workers. Also, even things sent in confidence to someone trusted can be used against the sender if relationships sour. It is worth advising your children to regard everything they send as capable of ending up being public. Warn them to deeply consider what they post about themselves.

Body image

In September 2021, a Facebook whistle blower, Frances Haugen's comments that the company's own research indicated their platform, particularly Instagram, was having a negative effect on teenagers. The *Wall Street Journal* printed an article about the deleterious effects of viewing Instagram posts including anxiety, depression and eating disorders like bulimia and anorexia nervosa. Thirty-two percent of teen girls in the study said if they had poor body image, they felt worse about themselves. And young men are not immune with 14% of them also feeling worse after viewing Instagram (Wells, Horowitz, & Seetharaman, 2021).

Instagram's head of public policy, Karina Newton commented in response saying that said the *Wall Street Journal* story had 'focused on a limited set of findings and casts them in a negative light'. I have some sympathy with Newton's statement, because researching the causality between social media on specific psychological and social outcomes is near impossible. It's difficult to use the data generated by social media research. A statistic can't capture the users' family and social environment or assess their mental states as they engage on these platforms. If we could assess these elements, it would greatly improve the interpretation of the data. But, even if we can't prove causality, we need to be aware of the issues.

When viewing social media platforms, children and young people are seeing everything from the outside. They cannot know the true circumstances or motives behind the posts. Not the real experiences, but a selection of the best of experiences are posted by celebrities and Instafamous people. Fear of missing out and envy of what kids perceive as others' amazing normal may impact on their self-worth. And their sense of inferiority is built on false, artificial exteriors.

The negative impact of social platforms may have harmful effects on self-esteem. Low self-esteem is proven to reduce quality-of-life outcomes because it blunts risk-taking, reduces resilience to bounce back from mistakes and causes people to become stuck in negative thinking spirals. Feelings of insignificance, loneliness, withdrawal and listlessness have teens feeling like they are walking through treacle. It can lead kids to make destructive decisions including accepting mistreatment, self-harming, promiscuity or harming others (Solomons, 2013).

It is important this information about damaging effects is in the public arena, but will it help your tweens and teens in the immediate term? Social media has outrun legislation, societal norms and user impact because it has happened so fast. Unlike mainstream journalism, norms and protocols for social media are in their infancy. It is not even certain if the platforms are publishers or not. As publishers, social media giants would be subject to entrenched laws, but their status as publishers is still being debated.

Quite simply we can't rely on social media platforms to solve the problem, we have to engage with it ourselves. It's time to transform the situation and create a narrative of using youthful minds and bodies to experience life and achieve unique personal goals and to shift the focus away from 'appearing' and start a revolution of 'doing'.

Parents have the power to influence this narrative from an early age, in fact, from infancy. What they say and how they say it can change how their children think. They can provide the activities that nurture a positive self-esteem. Thinking is the key to counteracting the powerful influences and manipulations emanating from social media.

How can we mitigate against the effects of social media?

As parents what you can do in the immediate term is work with your kids to hone social media literacy. We can help them to form a healthy balanced identity by applying advanced critical thinking. Good thinking can help them to navigate many of the deleterious influences that they will encounter.

360° Thinking

Converse with your family to develop perspectival, thinking. Offer different points of view. If you commence doing this from an early age, and pay attention to their perspectives during conversations, they are likely to see the value in this thinking.

Frame the experience by examining together how the images these days are photoshopped and manipulated to create near impossible ideals of body perfection. And before the photoshopping, kids are only choosing to portray their most enviable selves. The one selfie out of twenty that makes them look good.

Also talk about appearance as the least important part of a full life. Emphasise how the body is the vehicle for achievement in a million other ways.

Embrace directed by Taryn Brumfitt, founder of Body Image Movement, is a well-researched punch packing film that shines a light on the issue.

Taryn embarked on her film journey when she posted some reverse order photographs of herself. Her before image was her as a sculpted body builder, and her after image was taken when she had given birth to her baby. The photos caused a tsunami of negative comments. The film is her response, and every young person will learn from it (Brumfitt, 2016).

Presenting an optimistic view and offering realistic praise of their accomplishments can also counteract the effects of social media on their psyche.

Fake news
The same 360° thinking can arm your kids with the ability to filter out fake news. Remarkably, kids these days are more immune to the influence of fake news than we think they are. They are possible more alert than we are.

Develop face-to-face interests
As I write this, we are negotiating the roadmap out of intermittent COVID lockdowns in Victoria that have shaped the last 18 months. So truly there haven't been many opportunities for face-to-face anything!

But involving kids in team sports, rock climbing, dance, music, drama, writing, cooking, baking or strategy games like chess are all great ways for them to interact with real people in real situations. Having part-time jobs provides them with key skills that will come in handy later in life and look great on their CVs when they start looking for work seriously.

Gender and racial equality
Despite the publicity of issues related to gender and racial equality, they are pervasive in society and in the workplace. Attitudes and mindsets about others are formed very early on and generally children mirror what they observe in their role models. Many people are not even aware of their mindsets and act out automated attitudes. The family is a place

where conversations about the issues can inject understanding through perspective taking. Since her early teens, Candice has had a viewpoint on gender equality that broadened my mind and is worth sharing. She says, 'If you think feminism is a girl thing, you don't have the full picture. Every time you stereotype a girl, you stereotype a boy, or stereotype a someone. No-one on the planet should be pigeon-holed!'

Gender identity and sexual orientation
Thankfully in recent times, there is much more understanding about gender issues. But it is still not easy to support youngsters who do not fully identify with the gender type and expectations of their own body. Feelings of disconnect can arise from an early age and can evidence themselves at any time as children grow and develop. A friend's son made the decision to go through gender transformation hormone intervention and surgery in his mid-teens. He/she was one of the lucky ones whose parents both accepted, fully supported and financed this transformation and their relationship is rock solid. Sadly, this doesn't happen for all children who face issues. And even when families accept the situation, the kids might still have to deal with negativity from the school community and social networks around them. Added to the difficulties of coming to terms with dysphoria, anxiety, depression and other mental health issues may complicate the picture. This is one area where gaining access to professional support is advisable.

Anxiety and depression
No-one except sufferers of anxiety and depression can understand it. I recently watched a wonderful and traumatising series on TV called *Flowers*. The series follows the Flowers family, consisting of depressed father and children's writer, Maurice, music teacher wife, Deborah, their 25-year-old twin children: inventor son, Donald, mentally ill musician daughter, Amy, and Maurice's senile mother, Hattie. Added to this motley crew is Maurice's Japanese illustrator, Shun, with a tragic backstory. The writer and director, William Tomomori Fukuda Sharpe, Japanese-English actor, writer, and director who plays Shun has done a marvellous and

unsettling job of exploring the darkness of anxiety. It left me with a much deeper understanding of what it might feel like.

Research analysis by the University of Western Australia indicated that about 6.9% of children and adolescents surveyed have a diagnosed anxiety disorder, 4.3% experience separation anxiety and 2.3% have a social phobia (University of Western Australia, 2017). If the anxiety is advanced the children may be described as presenting with a mental disorder. A report after Naplan tests in Australia indicated that many students were suffering anxiety and even social phobia. A Telethon Kids research study indicates that students with poor mental health can be between seven to 11 months behind in year 3, and 1.5 – 2.8 years behind by year 9 (Telethon Kids, 2021). If educators or parents think their school children are in this category, they need to find professional support for the child, tween or teen.

Mind Share Partners reported that 50% of millennials and 75% of Gen Z-ers had left roles in the workplace for mental health reasons, both voluntarily and involuntarily (compared to 34% of overall respondents). Eighty-six percent of the survey respondents thought that a company's culture should support mental health (and even higher for millennials and Gen Z-ers). The most commonly desired workplace resources for mental health were trainings, clearer or more available information about where to go or who to ask for mental health support, and a more open culture about mental health at work (Mental Health at Work, 2019).

Foster care
I have never fostered children, so I have no experience of how foster families work. But I had the privilege of interviewing a father who had four children of his own and has fostered many children over the past 21 years. I will call the dad, Graham and his wife Anthea.

Graham wanted lots of kids, maybe six or eight. As life turned out he and Anthea had four. He'd reached a stage in life where the family was financially stable, had several properties and he was well established professionally. He was looking outwards to see how he could give back to community. It was Anthea who suggested foster care, so they embarked on the foster parent journey.

The reasons children find themselves in foster care are numerous and varied. Graham has fostered children for different periods of time and in different capacities. He and Anthea take children in emergencies for as little as a single night or week before placements are found. They've done permanent home care for two young girls which lasted for about 12 years. This means that they took full responsibility for them, including financial responsibility. Although this gave the foster parents and the foster sisters some security that they would stay together, once the relationship is permanent a lot of state support is withdrawn, including counselling sessions. It was not the financial situation, but the loss of the infrastructure that made Graham change tactics with later foster children. In later years, for three boys and a girl, the couple have opted to do long-term care, not permanent, because they have found the support from the state departments and private aid agencies to be immensely beneficial for the young people.

Some of the reasons children have come into their family are that a mother didn't want to keep her newborn baby, families have become dysfunctional through drug or alcohol use, physical and sexual abuse of children, and families not being in the financial health to support their children.

There is a difference between normal foster care and therapeutic foster care. Graham and Anthea do therapeutic care. With traditional foster care, parents must obtain 30 hours of pre-licensing training. For those providing therapeutic foster care, this increases to 37 hours of pre-licensing training. Therapeutic foster care parents also learn improved coping skills and how to manage some of the most challenging scenarios as part of training (UMFS, 2021). Graham has done the long hard yards and is respected by the foster services for the work he's done with his foster kids.

The most significant impact on children is a feeling of rejection. Graham explains that many of the kids he's fostered never felt connected. They never learned love and find it hard to accept love. They mistrust any efforts to make them feel happy. He explains how despite the mother of his first two young girls being known to them, the only time she wanted to see them was when she wanted to 'smoke drugs'. She'd call the girls to come over. They realised that this wasn't good for them, so they didn't go. However, when the mum died, both girls were devastated and felt guilty they hadn't spent more time with her. The door had permanently closed and they had a deep sense of loss. One of the girls also suffered an emotional breakdown when she discovered she and her sister didn't share the same father. She felt lied to and betrayed. She was furious with Graham for not telling her. He spoke to her honestly saying 'I am not on top of this. When should I tell you, when you're eight, when you're 12?' His own vulnerability shows in these statements. He says you can't always know exactly what to do, so you just do your best. He says that sometimes 'all the love in the world cannot pull the sorrow and rejection out of them'.

The worst Graham encountered was a child so traumatised by his early experiences between birth and four years of age, that he hadn't learned to speak. Not only a lack of language, but a lack of ability to understand how the world works at the simplest level, were missing when the boy arrived.

This bleak picture is countered by the fact that all six children Graham and Anthea took sole care or long-term responsibility for have made terrific progress. Some are already employed or running their own trades. Two are still living at home.

What are the elements that led children, one who couldn't talk and another who hid his face under a hoody to avoid eye contact, to be successful and productive?

Graham didn't list the strategies, but as I listened to him several factors became evident. He and Anthea listened to the children and were proactive when issues arose. If the children were being bullied at school, they did something about it. They attended scheduled round-table sessions with the clinicians and counsellors. They nutted out the issues, put solutions in place and followed up on advice. Graham admits to not following the advice to the letter sometimes, but he was the one living with the children and had immediate insight into what was working or not. Graham made the effort to keep in contact with any of the children's relatives if they showed an interest because he believes in maintaining their ties to their own families and communities despite the circumstances which has them living away from them. He treated the foster children exactly as his own. Same privileges, same remonstrations. He got all the kids into sports. He says his mates laugh at him because their kids are thirtyish now, and Graham is still taking two of his to Auskick! He doesn't just drop the children off. He stays and coaches the teams or watches from the sidelines. He swears by keeping children busy and socially connected. He and Anthea talk to the children all the time, no matter what their problems are.

Graham was clear that the training from the counselling services was very important in dealing with children's trauma. 'You can't approach that depth of pain without knowing what you're doing.' So, it was important to learn skills and to learn from lived experience.

One of the boys used to declare all the time that he was 'dumb'. He'd hardly start homework and say he was done. Graham was advised to focus on the child's interests and he loved sport, especially cricket. Graham would put the newspaper down casually open on the sports pages. The young man would look at it and recognise a sports' hero, grab the paper and do his best to read the scores and find out more about the celebrities. After several months the pathway to reading and learning opened for him.

The counselling also taught Graham and Anthea to understand the triggers of outbursts, harming, depressive episodes and rebellion that they had to deal with along the way. It gave them the skills to recognise signals, divert and pacify. He swears that humour is the best medicine. 'A bit of clowning goes a long way.'

He says the path of fostering is not easy. He had several bad experiences with short stay children. Often just as you get kids settled something happens and they have to leave. A court case closes and a biological parent rocks up to get the child. You know they are drug-affected and dealing, but you are helpless to object. A family member meddles in the situation and kids get removed from your family, returned home to a parent and end up being dropped off at a police station two weeks later because they still can't care for them.

Talking to Graham was humbling, inspiring and heartbreaking all at the same time. He says despite any difficulties and issues, it is one of the most rewarding things anyone can do. 'You take someone from total despair to totally different!' He still has contact with the baby who arrived when she was one day old and stayed for eight months. Now eight years old and happily adopted into the perfect family, she talks about her 'tummy mummy, her foster mummy and her forever mummy'.

Graham, Anthea and his biological children have made a world of difference to dozens of other children, including the long-term commitment to six of them. He is most certainly one of the 'I have your back' people in the world.

CHAPTER EIGHT

Forging a Family Culture

'Everything can be taken from a man but one thing; the last of the human freedoms – to choose one's attitude in any given set of circumstances, to choose one's own way.'
Viktor Frankl (1905–1997)
Psychiatrist and Holocaust survivor in *Man's Search for Meaning*

There are these two young fish swimming along and they happen to meet an older fish swimming the other way, who nods at them and says, 'Morning, boys. How's the water?' And the two young fish swim on for a bit, and then eventually one of them looks over at the other and goes 'What the hell is water?'

This story told by class representative, David Foster Wallace, at the Kenyon College US graduation in 2005 has become internationally famous. Wallace was saying that often the things that affect us most, are the most important to us, are invisible to us. The young fish are unaware of the substance that sustains their existence! One of these invisible things is culture.

I always understood culture as something transmitted down from those preceding us. Then during my education studies, I encountered the idea, that culture can be created. This completely new perspective excited me. It means that no-one is obliged to live out the patterns of the past. CEO of Reggio Children Carla Rinaldi and researcher Peter Moss describe culture as new learning:

> Learning is not the transmission of a defined body of knowledge [...] It is constructive, the subject constructing her or his own knowledge but always in democratic relationships with others and being open to different ways of seeing, since individual knowledge is always partial and provisional. From this perspective, learning is a process of constructing, testing and reconstructing theories, constantly creating new knowledge. [...] Learning itself is a subject for constant research ... (Rinaldi & Moss, 2004).

All families have a culture, even if they are completely unaware of it. Mostly they act out default family patterns. I encourage parents to embrace their power to forge a positive, unique family culture and identity. And there are many ways to do this.

Dancing with dolphins – choosing a family emblem

One of the things we did at the time of our departure from South Africa was create a family emblem. We chose the dolphin. A dolphin is both a sea creature and a mammal, and so is infinitely adaptable. It is comfortable in the wild and capable of thriving in captivity. It is strong, intelligent, beautiful and powerful. It swims vast distances, is social and playful. It can also be ferocious. But what we loved most about it was the ability to communicate with exquisite songs across great distances.

This emblem over the past 23 years has sustained us often. My own siblings and I regularly reference it in our conversations and it is part of our sibling 'tribalry'. We often sign off our messages with dolphins.

My brother, Martin, is a triathlete, and as I did when I was still a competitive racewalker, he uses the dolphin as way to strengthen his mindpower during performance. He imagines the strength of the dolphin, its exquisite rhythm and the cool sensation of swimming in the ocean.

My sister, Helene, has overcome deep personal tragedies in her life. She has a remarkable ability to keep moving. Currently she is renovating a three-storey, seven-bedroom villa south of Grenada in Spain. She too often taps into dolphin power as the enormity of the task sometimes seems overwhelming.

I use the image whenever I have something challenging to do. It has helped our nuclear and extended family to overcome distance in the past; and also now, during the COVID crisis, when my son resides in Sydney unable to visit us in Melbourne.

Emblems worked for families and communities in medieval times. They sustain communities today. I was honoured to hear an outstanding child psychologist, Winthrop Professor at the University of Western Australia, Dr Helen Milroy, talk at a conference in 2012 about how she uses totems as part of healing the experiences of traumatised, dislocated and distressed youth. Cultural stories, displaying the characteristic qualities animals and their negotiation of challenges, inspire, motivate and raise optimism. Story, image and totems give us pathways to understand our experience and ourselves.

Besides being a psychologist, Dr Milroy is an author and when asked in a newspaper interview in 2021 how stories can help children build courage, she answered that 'Storytelling is the oldest form of learning.' In Helen's own words:

> *We remember life through stories and learn so much from hearing other people's stories as well. This is true for children and adults. Stories can help children see different ways of understanding challenges and learning new ways to solve problems. It can help children see their unique place in the world and feel proud of who they are. It can help them see there is a solution and be inspired by others. (Lewis-Jones, 2021)*

Each of her characters is chosen because it emblemises some amazing human quality and teaches life lessons. You might select an emblem for your family or ask your child to choose their own personal emblem that captures qualities they would like to internalise for themselves. Then the emblems can inhabit, inspire and vitalise your family stories.

Holidays and holy days

Holidays are a time when the family spends more time than usual together. No matter whether the destination is a nearby camping site or an overseas trip, holidays are for making memories. The planning and anticipation are almost as important as the actual getaway! During holidays you get the opportunity to learn more about everyone and develop new skills and interests. Memories are family glue and holidays are the perfect way to make them.

Celebrating your religious, spiritual or national holidays is also a time to put your families unique stamp on events. What you do and how you do it, establishes traditions that can be repeated and even passed on down the generations. We always have our Christmas dinner on Christmas Eve.

I never saw the point in having a cooked dinner in the sweltering midday heat of a South African or Australian summer! The children got a Santa sock with an array of small gifts, one big present and usually a dressing up costume I'd made. One was a Ninja Turtle Sean wore to death and another was a butterfly costume that Candice, the entire Kindergarten community, and a cousin outgrew before it was sadly dispensed with 20 years later!

In the last 10 years, the emphasis has shifted to funny and gimmicky presents. Pierre recently received a mug from his adoring son. It read: 'Dear Dad, Thanks for putting up with a spoiled, messy, bratty child like my sister. Love, your favourite'. Pierre absolutely treasures it and we giggle every time he uses it. Last year Candice received a gift marked 'batteries included', and it was two batteries. (I had purchased a wall clock with a cat illustration on it for her vet practice that went with the batteries, but she only got that after New Year.)

Our family celebrates the arrival of spring with a special dinner. In the past it was roast lamb. Now we have a vegan and another who hates lamb! The ritual is wearing a jasmine crown. About three years ago I didn't plait the jasmine into crowns because I thought they'd well outgrown that, but there was an outcry that I'd changed the tradition. This year, 2021, we had to do it on zoom and even the brawny tattooed wore jasmine! The ritual bound us despite divisive debates the pandemic surfaced among us. We felt unified regardless of differing beliefs about the pandemic.

Families everywhere celebrate different events like Christmas, Thanksgiving, Shabbat or Diwali. There are cultural traditions of course, but it is fun to add your own family twist to the event.

And you can do the same for birthdays. We sometimes took the children and their friends to a venue, but mostly I arranged a party at home with a theme and a program of events. Scavenger hunts, athletics competitions, puppet shows, picnics and games are examples.

We also love celebrating decade birthdays with a lot of pomp and fun!

Some fun things you can try

Little letters

Pierre and I occasionally travelled without the children. If my dear mum, Bee, now departed, was available, she'd look after them. But several times we left the little critters with an au pair. One time, when the unsuspecting young lady arrived for a 10-day babysit, she found me washing Candi's hair with lice shampoo while Sean was looking at lice through a microscope in the garden. And I can tell you, we're lucky lice aren't the size of humans – because they are terrifying.

Fortunately the lice infestation was handled and the au pair was marvellous with the children.

But the thing I did to stay connected to the kids was leave them a letter for every day we were away.

The letters had generic news about where we were staying on that day and how we'd travelled there. If there was a local landmark, I'd describe it a bit. I would usually write a silly joke and tell them how much we loved them. The letters would 'arrive' in the post box each day. (Clearly the au pair had postage duties as well as babysitting.)

When Sean travelled overseas with Pierre, leaving Candice and me behind, I sent the letters with Pierre. I chose a 14-piece puzzle, and each day Sean would open a letter and get a piece. I made sure the pieces connected so he could see it growing and know how long it would be before we were together again.

When we moved to Melbourne, the kids had nine weeks out of school and we wanted them to carry on doing some academic work before attending their new schools. Because it was the first time we were in an ocean city, I chose King Neptune as a sender of nightly letters. They would turn up in the fruit bowl to be discovered in the morning. King Neptune's helper was Ariel and they dreamt up all kinds of projects for the children. They had to design a fashion show and work out a menu and shopping list for the event. There were mazes, sums, small writing tasks, obstacle courses and a host of small activities to keep their minds and bodies active. And I wasn't the one giving them any tasks!

A favourite one was a paper mural of South African and Australian animals. It turned out so successful I sent it to my mum in South Africa. She loved it and took it to be framed. The lady at the framers was impressed with the framed-up artwork and asked if she could keep it and display it in the gallery window for two weeks. When people saw the work in the window the shop had an instant demand for more framing of kids' art. So there we go, we started a trend 10,000 miles away! When we spoke about this recently, Candice said that long after King Neptune and Ariel had retired, she saw an envelope in the fruit bowl and opened it in great excitement only to discover that it was payment for our wonderful fortnightly cleaner.

Little tricks

There are some fun ways to frame children's experiences. When we were out hiking and the kids got tired of the trails and climbing up ridges, I would tell them stories. The focus on the plot, would shift their attention and they'd forget they weren't enjoying themselves. Sean also loved being a horse and 'pulling' me up the mountain. It was only years later we realised that his idea of a 'horse' was the cab of a big truck with a massive trailer, and mine was a traditional horse and cart!

I also bought rainbow-coloured shoelaces for their sneakers before the trip. They always thought they were magic.

Celebrate family achievements

Inspirational speakers, Stephen Covey and Brené Brown, both recommend being there to support all your family members' activities and achievements. To the extent you can, make sure you attend concerts, valedictories, matches and other sporting events. I have collected all the certificates and awards and intend putting a folder together to hand to Sean and Candice in the next year. Each of these mementos captures a moment when their persona, character and identity was being formed. Pierre and I are immensely proud of them as I am sure you are of your children's achievements as they enact their unique roles in this world.

AFTERWORD

Life as an Act of Creation

*'The art of progress is to reserve order amid change,
and to preserve change amid order.'*
Alfred North Whitehead

Potential of ingots

In the foreword I described the blacksmithing process whereby ingots are formed by pressing a workpiece amalgamated from carefully selected metals. An amalgam of our aspirations, values, resources and contributions to our children's future. The ingots contain all the latent potential of what they will become. From the ingot our children create their lives day by day.

A life of purpose fuelled with creative education, wrapped in loving communication and peppered with challenge is what I'm sure you wish for your kids as they negotiate their destiny. In the book *The Origins of You*, the authors continually distinguish between a deterministic future or a probabilistic future (Belsky, Caspi, Moffitt, & Poulton, 2020). They prefer the probabilistic because it is more open to positive influences. But I like to take it a step further. Dr Loretta Giurcelli, one of Australia's foremost educators, distinguishes between a probable and a preferred future. Not only a future more open to influence, but one where you go out of your way to provide positive influence.

Throughout this book the focus has been on creating a family milieu that encourages children to develop the autonomy to fly. Abraham Maslow's self-actualisation explains the qualities required to take flight. We've summarised his ideas in six words: self-regulation, self-esteem, self-purpose, self-mastery, creativity and contribution.

You've encountered ideas related to these words throughout this book as part of the greater vision for a resilient, high functioning family.

Your relationship with your children is a two-way street. You have plans for what they might do and how they'll turn out, but there will always be push back. I had anticipated that both my kids would attend university. Sean elected not to go that route. Initially Pierre and I were concerned about it. But over time, Sean has found the education that suits him and his aspirations. He engaged in self-development courses that gave him the skills and knowledge he needed. Sceptical at first, I now have a great respect for what he did and the people who managed the courses.

You won't know where your children are headed, however, you are instrumental in how they find their route and destination when you invest your attention and finances in their interests.

I focused a little on extracurricular activities in the first part of this book, but children learn completely different things out of school than in it.

In his great book, *Range*, David Epstein emphasises the importance of embracing a range of activities and experiences. I learnt heaps from my parents. My mother baked, sewed, gardened, flower-arranged, painted and drew. My dad worked, golfed, did carpentry, maintained vehicles and played the piano. Barring vehicle maintenance, I can pretty much do all of those things and I'm skilled with all kinds of tools. In my own career besides education, I dabbled in puppetry, flower arranging and fashion design. When I was appointed director of an early learning centre, suddenly I had all the skills that made me completely fit for purpose!

My kids picked up lots of skills from watching me and Pierre do stuff. This made them game to try anything! Sean built a computer called the 'Blue Beast' that is water-cooled and exudes an eerie blue light. He learnt how to construct it on the internet and imported parts from Poland. Candice, petite as she is, built a double-tier melamine enclosure for her two diamond pythons, Honey and Zeke. (I forgot to mention the snakes earlier. They only got lost in the house about six times.) She learned how to draft and build on the internet and had a couple of lessons from a boyfriend. I still see Sean with parts meticulously lined up, and Candi in the garage with protective eyewear and a power saw that made me retreat indoors because I couldn't watch her use it.

They both have great careers now. Candice is a veterinarian and Sean is a leading business professional in the retail industry. And they both have intriguing hobbies. Sean most recently built an adjustable timber desk with a beautiful, lacquered finish and backlighting. He also welded a small metal igloo shaped hot house. He did it all on the deck of his apartment! Candice sews and sells dog toys amongst a range of other crafts. Her latest project is intricate paper cut artworks which she designs, painstakingly cuts, mounts and frames. I never know what their next project will be.

You are who you were, you are who you are, you are who you're meant to be. You and your children never stop inventing themselves. My parents set me off on a road of lifelong learning. They appreciated my uniqueness, nurtured my talents and instilled a belief that I could create a worthy life. They gave me roots and wings. I dearly hope that Pierre and I have done the same for Sean and Candice. Wherever you are and whoever you are, I hope that you are being an 'I have' person for young people. A person who says, 'never fear, I have your back'.

Young people today have to field mass information from every corner of the planet. They may be called on to create their own career as entrepreneurship grows and long-term employment in standalone companies diminishes. But I believe we may underestimate how ready they are to take on the challenges of the future. I have witnessed my children follow their own paths and all I can say is that I have the greatest respect for how they think and what they've achieved.

At the start of the book I introduced the metaphor with a deliberate play on words of a mettle foundry, a workshop of creativity where a family's resilience is forged. There are hundreds of ways every day to bring cohesion to a family and to build resilience. A good education and well-crafted communication go a long way to forging a family with mettle.

The most important thing to forge is a golden thread of connection.

Sometimes you will feel the thread getting very thin. It might even be invisible, but as long as you feel its tug, as long as it doesn't break, your family will be whole. Beyond their own interests it is most likely you wish that your children live a life of contribution to others as well as to themselves. To reach a state of self-transcendence. As stated before, you can't be there for others, if you are not there for yourself.

I wish you well in your family. In the words of Marie Kondo, I hope that every moment you have together, even the ones that bring hard lessons, will 'spark joy'.

Tyger Tyger burning bright,

In the forests of the night:

What immortal hand or eye,

Dare frame thy fearful symmetry?

About the Author

Lili-Ann was born in Johannesburg, South Africa, and lived with her parents Bob and Bee Erasmus, and siblings Helene and Martin. Her father worked on the gold mines so the family relocated several times. As a child she loved spending time with her grandparents and on one of her visits, they went to a local fair. There were highland dancers performing and she loved it so much she immediately hopped up on stage with them! Consequently, she had her first ballet lesson at age four and she also loved piano lessons. Enid Blyton was her favourite author and she constantly entertained her siblings with her own made-up stories. When the family lived in Virginia, a country mining town, the children roamed freely in the neighbourhood. After school she would load her siblings onto a wooden wagon made by her grandpa and pull them into town to borrow books from the library. She has always loved going to the theatre and was mesmerised by puppet shows her primary teachers put on at school. All of these early influences continue to resonate in her life today.

Lili-Ann boarded at Eunice High School in Bloemfontein for her last two years of secondary school. After that she resided on campus at the University of the Witwatersrand to complete an education degree. During that time, she met Pierre, her husband, and they have made a wonderful life together with their son, Sean, and daughter, Candice. The family has travelled widely in Europe and America and skiing is their favourite holiday activity. Lili-Ann loves being active and what many don't know about her is that she earned Springbok national colours in South Africa for race walking!

The most significant and best decision the family made was to move to Australia in 1998.

Lili-Ann is passionate about education and completed a variety of courses culminating in a master's degree in education and leadership. Her life journey also included wonderful sidesteps into fashion design, floristry and puppetry.

During her career she has taught at all levels. In Melbourne, she had a sojourn at Bialik College and was Director of Early Learning at Fintona Girls' School for a decade. Her current role is a part-time education consultant at Independent Schools Victoria (ISV). Her time at ISV has afforded her many opportunities including becoming a trainer in Feuerstein Instrumental Enrichment, which focuses on human cognition. She also runs her own education consultancy, Kriegler-Education.

Apart from education, Lili-Ann is a keen golfer (some would say it is an addiction!). Her favourite place to play is at the home of golf, St Andrews in Scotland.

She enjoys Rotary and has been club president. One of most interesting Rotary endeavours was creating 'The Waggle Dance' to raise awareness about the global importance of bees and pollinators for food security. Many will know that bees do a waggle dance to communicate to their hive where to find pollen and nectar. Bees are vital for the planet and she and Pierre have a hive in their garden. Have a look at the World Bee Day website to watch the dance or upload your own!

She loves spending time with friends and family, especially visiting her siblings in the UK and Spain.

Lili-Ann plans to continue working as an education consultant. Her education business, Kriegler-Education is growing and she is loving the journey of meeting new educators and taking on new challenges.

To get in touch with Lili-Ann, visit her website: https://www.kriegler-education.com

Acknowledgements

Where do you start to acknowledge everyone who makes your work and your challenge a reality? There are so many people who have influenced my thinking, my career and my aspirations. I start by thanking my husband for his constant support, incisive comments, forward propulsion and patience. Pierre you are without a doubt, the 'wind beneath my wings'. I acknowledge my miraculous and amazing adult children, Sean and Candice. I thank you for your enthusiastic interest in all my endeavours. (Even the crazy ones!)

I am grateful to my late parents, Bob and Bee, for instilling a lifelong belief in the power of education and for their encouragement and support. Likewise, to my siblings, Helene and Martin, who have achieved great things in their lives based on the same foundations.

I thank all the colleagues I have worked with since I started my career in South Africa and in my time working in this enviable country, Australia. I have learned with you and from you every day as we enacted our roles shoulder to shoulder.

I would like to make a special mention of two valued mentors, Jan Millikan OAM and Genia Janover. Your contribution to me personally and to education in general cannot be quantified.

Professional learning is mandated for educators, and I have participated in so many important programs throughout my career. But two of these journeys need to be highlighted. The knowledge I have gained from my encounters with the Reggio Emilia philosophy and the education absorbed from the Feuerstein Institute have been game changers for me.

To the team at Ultimate 48 Hour Author, your professionalism, knowledge, support and wisdom has made my authoring journey infinitely more achievable and I thank you all.

To all my friends and family spread far and wide, your interest and support is greatly appreciated.

SPEAKER BIOGRAPHY
LILI-ANN KRIEGLER

'I BELIEVE IN THE TRANSFORMATIVE POWER OF EDUCATION'

Lili-Ann Kriegler (B. A Hons, H. Dip. Ed, M.Ed.) is a Melbourne-based education consultant and author of 'Edu-Chameleon' and 'Roots and Wings'. Lili-Ann's specialisations are in early childhood education (birth-9 years), leadership and optimising human thinking and cognition. Her current part-time role is as an education consultant at Independent Schools Victoria and she runs her own consultancy, Kriegler-Education. Lili-Ann is a child, parent and family advocate who believes that education is a positive transformative force for humanity. Find out more at https://www.kriegler-education.com

PRESENTATIONS

Lili-Ann offers talks for parents and educators about a variety of topics to promote children's optimum development and learning. She encourages parents to embrace their power to create a positive family culture. Her talks are peppered with anecdotes from years of experience. Lili-Ann says families, in all their infinite variety, play a significant role in shaping a preferred future of society, one they would love their children to live in.

TESTIMONIAL

Lili-Ann's knowledge and understanding of education, particularly early years, is vast. She explores the links between emotion and cognition. She seeks every opportunity to contribute to current research and further best practice. This, combined with her deep understanding and expertise in teaching, makes her an outstanding educator.

Genia Janover, Past Principal of Bialik College
Ambassador and Principal Advisor at Independent Schools Victoria

Email: lili-ann@kriegler-education.com; or visit www.kriegler-education.com to make a booking.
Mobile: +61-438489032

References

AFP. (2020, February 13). *Australian-first research finds most parents do not think online sexual exploitation can happen to their child.* Australian Federal Police. https://www.afp.gov.au/news-media/media-releases/australian-first-research-finds-most-parents-do-not-think-online-sexual

A Mug To Keep Designs. (2021, Dec 3). *Funny Mug.* Amazon. https://www.amazon.com/Funny-Mug-putting-favorite-Inspirational/dp/B01FAZZEAA

Atherton, F., & Nutbrown, C. (2013). *Understanding Schemas and Young Children – Birth to Three.* SAGE.

Baum, D. (2018, February 4). *The Power of Walking Conversations.* David Baum: https://www.davidbaum.com/news/2018/2/4/the-power-of-walking-conversations

Belsky, J., Caspi, A., Moffitt, T. E., & Poulton, R. (2020). *The Origins of You – How Childhood Shapes Later Life.* Harvard University Press.

Bowlby, J. (1977). The Making and Breaking of Affectional Bonds. *The British Journal of Psychiatry, 130*(3), 201–210.

Bronfenbrenner, U. (1979). *The Ecology of Human Development.* Harvard University Press.

Bronson, P., & Merryman, A. (2009). *NurtureShock.* Twelve, Hatchette Book Group.

Brumfitt, T. (Director). (2016). *Embrace* [Motion Picture]. Southern Light Alliance.

Bruner, J. (1983). *Child's Talk*. Norton and Comapany Limited.

Buzan, T. (2010). *Use Your Head – how to unleash the power of your mind*. Pearson Education.

Carter, H. (1953). *Where Main Street Meets the River*. Rinehart & Company.

Christakis, E. (2021, June 18). *The Dangers of Distracted Parents*. The Atlantic. https://www.theatlantic.com/magazine/archive/2018/07/the-dangers-of-distracted-parenting/561752/

Clinton Foundation. (2021, June 23). Too Small to Fail. https://www.clintonfoundation.org/programs/education-health-equity/too-small-fail/

Covey, S. R. (2014). *7 Habits of Highly Effective Families*. St Martin's Press.

Donaldson, M. (1984). *Children's Minds*. Fontana.

Edwards, C., Gandini, L., & Foreman, E. G. (Eds.). (1998). *The Hundred Languages of Children: The Reggio Emilia Approach advanced perspectives*. Ablex Publishing Corporation.

Epstein, R. H. (2019, August 21). *Why More Kids Are Starting Puberty Earlier Than Ever Before*. Psychology Today. https://www.psychologytoday.com/au/articles/201908/why-more-kids-are-starting-puberty-earlier-ever

Faber, A., & Mazlish, E. (1980). *How to Talk so Kids Will Listen and Listen so Kids Will Talk*. Simon and Schuster.

FACT Dr. (2021, June 13). *Anal Sex: Tips from experts on how to be kinky yet safe*. https://factdr.com/sexual-health/anal-sex-tips/.

Fandom. (2021, June 23). *Orange Is the New Black Wiki*. https://orange-is-the-new-black.fandom.com/wiki/Maria_Ruiz

Farah, M., Sternberg, S., Nichols, T.A., Duda, J.T., Lohrenz, T., Luo, Y., Sonnier, L., Ramey, S.L., Montague, R., & Ramey, C.T. (2021). Randomized Manipulation of Early Cognitive Experience Impacts Adult Brain Structure. *Journal of Cognitive Neuroscience, 33*(6) 1197–1209.

Feuerstein, R., Rand, Y., Hoffman, M., & Miller, R. (1980). *Instrumental Enrichment: An Intervention Program for Cognitive Modifiability*. Scott, Foresman & Co.

Flood San Diego. (2021, October 12). *The Marshmallow Experiment – Instant Gratification*. Retrieved from YouTube. https://theforeveryears.wordpress.com/2016/11/08/the-dunedin-study-the-vital-importance-of-self-control-in-creating-positive-life-outcomes-by-kirsteen-mclay-knopp/

Fox, M. (2008). *Reading Magic – Why Reading Aloud to Our Children Will Change Their Lives Forever.* Simon and Schuster .

Fox, M. (2013, September 26). *Ten read-aloud commandments.* Mem Fox. https://memfox.com/for-parents/for-parents-ten-read-aloud-commandments/

funnyplox. (2021, June 21). *babies babble on phones.* [Video]. YouTube. https://www.youtube.com/watch?v=YqcFJfoVFM0&ab_channel=funnyploxfunnyplox

Goldstein, M. H., Waterfall, H. R., Lotem, A., Halpern, J. Y., Schwade, J. A., Onnis, L., & Edelman, S. (2010). General Cognitive Principles for learning Structures in Time and Space. *Trends in Cognitive Sciences, 14*(6), 233–290.

Golinkoff, R. M. (2015). (Baby)Talk to Me: The Social Context of Infant-Directed Speech and Its Effects on Early Language Acquisition. *APS Association of Pshychological Science,* https://doi.org/10.1177/0963721415595345.

Gould, T. J. (2010). Addicition and Cognition. *Addiction Science and Clinical Practice, 5*(2), 4–14.

Greenfield, S. (2015). *Mind Change – How digital technologies are leaving their mark on our brains.* Random House.

Hart, B., & Risley, T. R. (1995). *Meaningful Differences in the Everyday Experience of Young American Children.* Paul H Brookes PublishingCo.

Hebb, D. (1949). *The Organization of Behaviour: a neuropshcyoloigal theory.* Wylie.

Hill, N. (2019). *Think and Grow Rich.* Penguin.

Horvath, J. C. (2019). *Stop talking and start influencing.* Exisle Publishing.

James, W. (1890). *The Principles of Psychology.* (Chapter 8). An internet resource developed by Christopher D Green. https://psychclassics.yorku.ca/James/Principles/prin13.htm

Johnson, D. E., Guthrie, D., Smyke, A. T., Koga, S. F., Fox, N. A., Zeanah, C. H., & Nelson, C. A. (2010). Growth and associations between auxology, caregiving environment, and cognition in socially deprived Romanian children randomized to fosters vs ongoing institutional care. *Archives of Paediatric & Adolescent Medicine, 164*(6), 507–516.

Leach, P. (1977). *Baby and Child.* Michael Joseph Limited.

Lewis-Jones, M. (2021, April 4). *Lofty lifts off – an interview with Helen Milroy.* Sydney Morning Herald. https://southsydneyherald.com.au/lofty-lifts-off-and-conveys-life-lessons-for-children/

Markland, A. D., Dunivan, G. C., Vaugan, C. P., & Rogers, R. G. (2016, February). Anal Intercourse and Fecal Incontinence: Evidence from the 2009–2010 National Health and Nutrition Examination Survey. *American Journal of Gastroenterology, 111*(2), 269–274. https://www.ncbi.nlm.nih.gov/pmc/articles/PMC5231615/

Maslow, A. H. (2017). *A Theory of Human Motivation*. BN Publishing.

Medina, J. (2014). *Brain Rules*. Scribe Publications .

Mind Share Partners. (2019). *Mental Health at Work*. (2019). https://www.mindsharepartners.org/mentalhealthatworkreport-download

Mischel, W. (2015). *The Marshmallow Test – Mastering Self Control*. Transworld Publishers.

Nall, R. (2019, March 6). *What are the risks of anal sex?* Medical News Today. https://www.medicalnewstoday.com/articles/324637

News.com.au. (2019, October 24). *'If it wasn't for that, he'd be here': 21yo dies after gambling spiral*. https://www.news.com.au/lifestyle/real-life/if-it-wasnt-for-that-hed-be-here-21yo-dies-after-gambling-spiral/news-story/f7ec6ee6edbd74ce5958cf677c36638b

Orthopedics North West. (2021, September 26). *Hand Anatomy*. https://www.orthonw.com/hand-anatomy-orthopedics-northwest-tigard-oregon.html

Oxford University Press.(2021) mettle. In: Lexico.com. https://www.lexico.com/definition/mettle [Accessed 17/02/2022].

Quadara, A., El-Murr, A., & Latham, J. (2017) *The effects of pornography on children and young people*. Australian Government – Australian Institute of Family Studies. https://aifs.gov.au/publications/effects-pornography-children-and-young-people

Reid, J., & Low, J. (1977). *The Written Word*. Holmes McDougall.

Rinaldi, C. (2001). The Pedagogy of Listening. *Innovations in early education: the international reggio exchange, 8*(4).

Rinaldi, C., & Moss, P. (2004). What is Reggio?. In *Children in Europe: Celebrating 40 years of Reggio Emilia – the pedagogical thought and practice underlying the world renowned early services in Italy* (p2).

Robert, T. K. (2017). *Rich Dad Poor Dad - what the rich teach their kids about money that the poor and middle class do not!* Plata Publishing.

Routledge, C. (2016, November). *Why do we feel nostalgia?* Ted-Ed: https://www.ted.com/talks/clay_routledge_why_do_we_feel_nostalgia/transcript

Santer, D. (Exceutive Producer). (2016–2018). *Flowers* [TV series]. Channel 4.

Schonkoff, J.P. (2021, June 21). *A Guide to Serve and Return: How Your Interaction with Children Can Build Brains*. Center on the Developing Child – Harvard University. https://developingchild.harvard.edu/guide/a-guide-to-serve-and-return-how-your-interaction-with-children-can-build-brains/

Schonkoff, J. P., Phillips, D. A., & (Eds). (2000). *From Neurons to Neighbourhoods – The science of early childhood development*. The National Academy of Sciences.

Senge, P. (2006). *The Fifth Discipline – The Art and Practice of Learning Organisations*. Century Trade.

Shelby Church. (2021, July 5). *Wandering in the Snow*. The Church at Shelby Crossings. https://shelbycrossings.com/2013/02/wandering-in-the-snow/

Shore, R. (1997). *Rethinking the Brain*. Families and Work Institute.

Solomons, K. (2013). *Born to be Worthless: The Hidden Power of Low Self-Esteem*. Create Space Indpenedent Publishing Platform.

Steven, K. (2021). *The Art of the Impossible*. Harper Collins.

Stipek, D., & Seal, K. (2001). *Motivated Minds: Raising Children to Love Learning*. Henry Holt.

Summerton, R., Hyde, S., & Scott, L. (Producers). (2019). *The Hunting*. [TV series]. Closer Productions.

Suskind, D. (2015). *Thirty Million Words – Building a Child's Brain*. Dutton.

Terlizzi, J. (2021, November 24). *A Doctor's Guide to Bottoming*. Lighthouse LGBTQ + Affirming Care. https://blog.lighthouse.lgbt/doctors-guide-to-bottoming/

Think U Know. (2021, October 12). *Preventing online child sexual exploitation*. http://www.thinkuknow.org.au/

Tronick, D. E. (2021, June 21). *Still Face Experiment*. Retrieved from YouTube: https://www.youtube.com/watch?v=apzXGEbZht0&ab_channel=UMassBoston

Tronick, E. (2009, December 1). *Still Face Experiment: Dr. Edward Tronick*. [Video]. YouTube. https://www.youtube.com/watch?v=apzXGEbZht0&ab_channel=UMassBoston

UMFS. (2021, November 10). *Therapeutic vs. Traditional Foster Care*. https://www.umfs.org/therapeutic-vs-traditional-foster-care/

University of Western Australia. (2017). *Child and Adolescent Mental Health and Educational Outcomes - An analysis of educational outcomes from Young Minds Matter: the second Australian Child and Adolescent*

Survey of Mental Health and Wellbeing. https://youngmindsmatter.telethonkids.org.au/siteassets/media-docs---young-minds-matter/childandadolescentmentalhealthandeducationaloutcomesdec2017.pdf

Vance, J. D. (2016). *Hillbilly Elegy*. Harper Collins Publishers Limited.

Vertava Health. (2021, October 2). *Understanding the Jellinek Curve of Addiction*. https://vertavahealth.com/blog/jellinek-curve-of-addiction/

Wallace, D. F. (2021, December 3). *This water by David Foster Wallace*. Farnam Street. https://fs.blog/david-foster-wallace-this-is-water/

Wells, G., Horowitz, J., & Seetharaman, D. (2021, September 14). *Facebook Knows Instagram Is Toxic for Teen Girls, Company Documents Show*. Wall Street Journal: https://www.wsj.com/articles/facebook-knows-instagram-is-toxic-for-teen-girls-company-documents-show-11631620739

Whitehouse, A., Green, J., & Hudry, K. (2021, September 21). *Therapy fo babies showing early signs of autism reduces the chance of clinical diagnosis at age 3*. The Conversation. https://theconversation.com/therapy-for-babies-showing-early-signs-of-autism-reduces-the-chance-of-clinical-diagnosis-at-age-3-167146?utm_source=linkedin&utm_medium=bylinelinkedinbutton

Wikipedia. (2021, November 24). *Abraham Maslow*. https://en.wikipedia.org/wiki/Abraham_Maslow#cite_note-50:

Witherow, T. (2021, October 2). *Young people are NINE times more likely to attempt suicide if they are problem gamblers, study finds*. Daily Mail: https://www.dailymail.co.uk/news/article-9230269/Young-people-NINE-times-likely-attempt-suicide-problem-gamblers-study-finds.html

Young Minds Matter (2021). *Educational Outcomes*. https://youngmindsmatter.telethonkids.org.au/NAPLAN

Notes

www.ingramcontent.com/pod-product-compliance
Lightning Source LLC
Chambersburg PA
CBHW071607080526
44588CB00010B/1054